Selling to Anyone Over the Phone

SECOND EDITION

D0062059

Selling to Anyone Over the Phone

SECOND EDITION

Renee P. Walkup with Sandra McKee

AMACOM

AMERICAN MANAGEMENT ASSOCIATION
New York • Atlanta • Brussels • Chicago • Mexico City • San Francisco
Shanghai • Tokyo • Toronto • Washington, D.C.

Bulk discounts available. For details visit:
www.amacombooks.org/go/specialsales
Or contact special sales:
Phone: 800-250-5308
Email: specialsls@amanet.org

View all the AMACOM titles at: www.amacombooks.org

This publication is designed to provide accurate and authoritative information in regard to the subject matter covered. It is sold with the understanding that the publisher is not engaged in rendering legal, accounting, or other professional service. If legal advice or other expert assistance is required, the services of a competent professional person should be sought.

Library of Congress Cataloging-in-Publication Data
Walkup, Renee P., 1957-
    Selling to anyone over the phone / Renee P. Walkup with Sandra McKee.
— 2nd ed.
        p. cm.
    Includes index.
    ISBN-13: 978-0-8144-1483-5 (pbk.)
    ISBN-10: 0-8144-1483-4 (pbk.)
    1.   Telephone selling.   I. McKee, Sandra L., 1952- II. Title.
    HF5438.3.W34 2011
    658.8'72—dc22

                                                                    2010006636

© 2011 Renee P. Walkup

All rights reserved.

Printed in the United States of America.

This publication may not be reproduced, stored in a retrieval system, or transmitted in whole or in part, in any form or by any means, electronic, mechanical, photocopying, recording, or otherwise, without the prior written permission of AMACOM, a division of American Management Association, 1601 Broadway, New York, NY 10019.

About AMA

American Management Association (www.amanet.org) is a world leader in talent development, advancing the skills of individuals to drive business success. Our mission is to support the goals of individuals and organizations through a complete range of products and services, including classroom and virtual seminars, webcasts, webinars, podcasts, conferences, corporate and government solutions, business books, and research. AMA's approach to improving performance combines experiential learning—learning through doing—with opportunities for ongoing professional growth at every step of one's career journey.

Printing Number

10   9   8   7   6   5   4   3   2   1

Contents

Negotiate: Carve Out the Details

Seal the Close

The Payoff

The Pros and Cons of New Technology

Guidelines for the Strategic Use of New Technology

The Payoff

The Importance of Time

The Role of the Relationship

Language and Communication Across Cultures

Culture and Personality

Dealing with Cultural Differences

The Payoff

Acknowledgments

SANDRA MCKEE would like to acknowledge the brilliance and un-flagging enthusiasm (and occasional nagging) of coauthor Renee Walkup during the development of this book. She also thanks business clients and students who have affirmed, by their progress and feedback, the methods that appear here.

And speaking of nagging, **RENEE WALKUP** would like to thank Sandra McKee for helping me to make this book a reality. Sandra, you are an inspiration and you never fail to impress me with your skills as a talented writer and storyteller. I would also like to thank my hundreds of clients for their trust and support over these last thirteen years since founding SalesPEAK. You are the people who charge me up in the morning and throughout every day.

To my husband, Ted, thank you for all you do to support me in my work, and also to my daughter, Rachel, for your patience with my time spent on this project. Thank you both!

Both **RENEE AND SANDRA** are grateful to Bob Nirkind, senior acquisitions editor at AMACOM Books, for his enthusiasm for our project. Rarely do authors have the opportunity to work with an editor who exhibits the level of expertise and professionalism that Bob has shown. His diligence and vision were instrumental in making this book what it is.

We also want to thank our copyeditor, Debbie Posner; Associate Editor/Copy Manager Erika Spelman; and the editorial and production staff of AMACOM. You listened to our suggestions and then made this the best book it could be.

Introduction:
Selling "Double Green"

Years ago, our entrepreneurial ancestors pushed a cart through the city square to peddle their wares. And the profession of "sales" was born.

The interactions were in person. Face to face. And although many a peddler burned untold calories pushing his cart around, he left no effect on the environment in his wake. Since then, many sales evolutions have taken place. John Deere and his wagon loaded with plows led to the more modern day with hundreds of thousands of salespeople on the road driving millions of miles each year to visit customers. These numbers have steadily risen over time.

With the advent of better train and air travel, we've added driving to stations and airports, hopping on trains as well as planes—just so we could meet with our customers in person, hoping to close the sale. And we have been very successful with this method in the past. But consider this: It costs a company between $100 and $600 dollars for a salesperson to visit a single customer in person (depending, of course, on how close together customers are clustered).

A new day has dawned in sales, and with it has come rising travel costs, increased wait times, and a lower return on investment for individual sales staff because of the time/money trade-off. Time spent on planes is not generating revenue. Time spent waiting to see customers can also eat into return on sales investment because it's not direct customer contact time. Not only does selling on the phone virtually eliminate these concerns, it adds the bonus of being a more *green* method of selling.

Or, looking at this another way, the ROI of using the telephone to sell is far more profitable for companies. More salespeople can be employed, less waste takes place, and business gets back on track for profitability.

One of our clients began an inside sales organization employing six telephone salespeople in 1994. Her group's sales grew to around $500,000 the first year they were in operation. Today, she employs over eighty inside salespeople and their sales have grown to over $100 million! Her departmental costs are a fraction of the outside sales organization's. Every salesperson has a desk and a telephone. Her salespeople can make dozens of sales calls per day, as compared to outside reps, who can make a maximum of only ten sales calls daily.

Senior management at this company is thrilled with their results. Our client's employees consistently win the sales awards at national meetings, outselling and outproducing the salespeople who are also using more of our earth's resources to accomplish sales. In short, the company achieves a dramatically better ROI for their inside sales team than for their outside sales force.

Hence the "double" in "double green"—greener to the planet, and more green in your pocket.

While you're taking a more responsible stance toward the future of the planet by utilizing the telephone more effectively and minimizing travel costs, you may be wondering why customers prefer to conduct business over the telephone as well. The answer is simple. *Time.* All customers have a limited amount of time to work with salespeople. If you've ever heard "I'm just too busy" from a customer, and you believe there is sincerity behind those words, then you understand.

Meeting with a sales rep in person means that the customer has to carve out valuable time away from daily job demands. A phone call is less time-consuming for him or her, and just as effective for you (if not more so), than that one-hour face-to-face appointment. With a focused call, most trained salespeople can accomplish their call goal in a quarter of the time it would normally take to meet with the customer in person.

In this Second Edition of *Selling to Anyone Over the Phone* we explore how you can maximize your sales, save operating expenses, and operate "in the green" by using the telephone. Instead of just telling you to "call, call, and call," we explain how you can *effectively* use the phone to generate business.

In this book you will learn the tips and finer points of phone selling as you become more skillful at using the phone to:

- Focus the customer's attention on your call.
- Engage customers in conversation and keep them there.
- Generate interest in your products/services.
- Not only get past gatekeepers but also gain their help to reach your customer.
- Ensure callbacks from customers.
- Set appointments and prevent customers from canceling them.
- Conduct webinars and conference calls with multiple decision makers.
- Utilize communication technology to go "global."

Plus, new to this edition you'll find:

- A new chapter on presenting to groups over the phone via webinars and teleconferences.
- New information on outside salespeople transitioning to inside phone sales.
- New material on establishing trust relationships over the phone.
- Guidelines for the use of text messaging.
- Expanded coverage on global and cross-cultural communication.
- New phone selling challenges to open each chapter.
- New models of effective and ineffective telephone exchanges between salesperson and customer.
- A new "Greener Way to Do Business" sidebar in each chapter discussing ways in which doing business over the phone is environmentally friendly.

- New "Talk Tip" sidebars throughout the book.
- A new appendix on handling customer complaints.

And by the end of the book, you will definitely know how to make more sales, increase your bank account, and contribute to a cleaner world, all by selling to *anyone* over the phone!

CHAPTER 1

Setting Up for Success

PHONE SALES CHALLENGE – *Linda, who was recently moved inside after calling on medical offices as a drug rep, tells us: "I know I should be calling more, but I just can't make myself get on the phone."*

Linda probably can't get going because she's tired of being a loser. Perhaps that's harsh but, come on, does anybody hate making money? She has likely fallen into some lame patterns that take her nowhere, such as these openings, which don't engage the customer:

- "How are you?"
- "I wanted to tell you about our company's offerings."
- "I'm glad I caught you because we have some specials that I wanted to share with you."

You can blame the economy, the competition, or your company's marketing department. But the reality is this: There are people out there making money selling over the phone and *you* need to be one of them.

Apply New Tactics for New Times

Whether you have always been in phone sales or have recently been pulled in from the road to cut company expenses, it's time to retrain. Competition is brutal, the country's finances have been on a roller-coaster ride, and customers are more stressed in general. Whatever tricks you've used that have worked in the past may very well be your worst enemy today. If you're already a seasoned phone rep, it could be your compelling voice, your energy level, or your sense of humor. If you've been in personal contact selling, it might be your killer smile, your uncanny ability to read faces or body language, or your laptop full of data.

Do these statements seem odd? Are you asking yourself, "Who doesn't like a killer smile? A sense of humor? What's wrong with these authors?" Read on.

THROW OUT THE OLD

It's a new phone selling environment, so many of the old ways, even your favorites, probably need to be retired to make way for more effective approaches. Here are a few that you will want to send to the recycle bin.

Seduction. You use charisma, compliments, and maybe even a little on-the-phone flirtation to form a quickly intimate connection. Come on, you know you've done this. Don't be embarrassed. Whole books are written to teach people seduction tactics and you just do it naturally. It doesn't matter if it's a business deal, a better rate at the hotel, or a date for the evening, you are a master at getting what you want—given willingly—as long as the client is susceptible to a smooth line.

Databank. Employing this approach, you push long lists of product features through the phone lines in order to cover the customer in information. When enough positive features about your product—followed by some dirt thrown on the competition—have overwhelmed (some would say "battered") your customer, he or she quickly says "yes." Unfortunately, luck has to play a big part. Either the client hears something early on that strikes a chord, or all the excess talk results in you talking yourself out of a sale.

Big Dog. Using this psychological tactic, you make it clear that you are a force to be reckoned with, with agreement the customer's only option. Your resounding voice booms into the customer's ear, overpowering the weak-willed. This works enough of the time to keep you using it; it just doesn't work on everyone, though, and it generally only works when the customer has no immediate escape route. Businesspeople hear enough of this from used car ads on the radio. They certainly don't want to be harangued over their phone as well. Hangups are too easy.

Infusion. Your enthusiasm and passion can go a long way toward infusing a customer with eagerness for your product. If you generate energy at a high enough level, you can almost compel the buyer to vibrate with you on the other end of the phone. Even if you are naturally a hyper personality or are genuinely excited about your company's products, that high level of fervor is impossible to maintain all day every day. The limitation is that you are generally effective only on "good" days. In addition, you run the risk of quickly exhausting the customer who's having a bad day, resulting again in (you guessed it) a hang-up.

Glad Hand. Your "never met a stranger I didn't like" approach ensures that clients will look forward to your phone "visits" (note the use of that particular word). You love engaging new prospects, getting to know them, and learning what they're into. You're generally a good listener and probably have made some personal phone friends of your customers along the way. When all things are equal, you get the business because they feel they know you. The kick in the gut comes when the voice on the phone says, "You know I like you, Keith, but the other company had more of what we needed. I'm real sorry. Next time I'll try to throw some business your way." People like their friends, but they buy from those who can solve their problems.

BRING IN THE NEW

As you can see from the examples above, most of the "wins" occurred only when the particular customer situation matched your sales style. None of these approaches on their own is effective over time, and rarely do they translate immediately into success on the phone. Strategic phone selling tactics can dramatically increase your close rate and you won't even have to leave your office.

Whatever you consider your strength, it could be turning you into a "one-trick pony." Not the cute little ones that everyone loves, but the kind of salesperson who can only get customers through a natural rapport. In these challenging times, you need to get all the customers, not just the ones that you click with naturally.

To do this, you are going to have to use that extra-sharp brain that made you successful in the first place, but you will be using it to apply new tactics that will close sales with *any* customers. There's only so far you can go trying to dazzle busy, stressed-out customers with your wit or charm. Did you know that in the movie *Hidalgo*, six different horses were used to perform the different actions the scenes required? Each horse did only one trick well.

You're not a horse! It's time for you to move from one-trick pony to morph master, able to size up a customer situation and whip out a tactic perfectly matched to that customer. If you can't make the customers believe that you and your product are credible solutions to their problems, then you become just another stressor in their already stressful day. But when you hit that sweet spot, that balance between listening to and engaging the customer, you can almost smell the money.

Move to Phone Selling Success

Outside salespeople may be reluctant to move away from the security of their surefire, face-to-face winning ways. But the reality is that the cost of travel is increasing—even just across town—and there is a pressing need to generate more dollars out of every minute of sales time. More and more salespeople will be moved inside to the phone, and you will probably be among them (if you're not there already).

> ### A Greener Way to Do Business
>
> According to goldcalltraining.com, an outbound sales call costs only between $13 and $19, depending on the salesperson's compensation. Data from the McGraw-Hill Company confirms that the cost of each face-to-face call is at least $347 for a medium-size business, and this number continues to escalate. If we looked at the carbon footprint of all the driving, the price tag for the planet further increases the cost. Phone selling is green-green: good for the environment and good for the company's bottom line.

Does phone selling scare you?

Very few people who are in sales for a living have not had to address the fear of what might happen if he or she "chokes" during a performance (sales call). Even the most experienced longtime professionals have days where calling, especially prospecting, is stressful. But when you have a plan that is likely to result in success, you look forward to the call experience, and your stress is reduced.

Think of it this way. If you have good skills in basketball, don't you welcome the chance to demonstrate them in a game? When you raise your skill level and learn to manage all types of calls, a call then becomes another opportunity to be successful. This chapter is about developing a solid phone strategy.

Imagine that your goals are in place and you are confident, motivated, and prepared for success. Now read on to learn how you can start each of your sales days with success, instead of just coffee!

Begin Your Prep Work

It's wise to do all your preparatory work the day or evening before your call day. If you wait to plan after you have begun your workday, you've already fallen behind! Preparation saves time and maximizes your opportunities for a successful day of contacts and closes. To plan ahead, you need to:

- Organize your work space.
- Set your call goals.
- Prioritize your call times.

ORGANIZE YOUR WORK SPACE

An important piece of prep work that many salespeople forget is the preparation of the work space. In addition to paper pileups, computer tools are constantly notifying us of messages and work that must be done. Turn off your email message beeper and other audible tools that create distractions. Remember: Your customer is the most important person on the planet during your call. That person is where your focus must be.

SET YOUR CALL GOALS

Start with a plan for contacting three times *more* customers than you think is humanly possible. If your expectations are that you should make thirty contacts a day, then plan on ninety calls. At least 75 percent of those calls are going to result in your leaving a voice mail message, which generally takes no more than thirty seconds. These will be strategic communications left for decision makers on their phone message systems—important but not time-consuming. Know in advance exactly what message you are going to leave. Some may find it helpful to write it out and rehearse it until it sounds relaxed and natural. In one hour, with good planning, you should easily get in thirty outbound call messages.

Of course, if you spend five hours of your day actually talking to customers and closing business, no one will ever be concerned that you never reached ninety calls. The key is to ensure that you are making the most productive use of your time as possible. Have enough phone numbers and strategy notes in front of you for an entire call day.

Have strategy notes before you punch in those numbers. Strategy notes allow you to hold all the cards in a phone conversation. When you plan ahead with a specific approach customized for the client you are calling, you are the one in control. If you are making ninety calls a day, you can't possibly remember every strategic detail of every call in your plan. Strategy notes keep you on target and calm—in other words, you never call anyone without being ready to do business. This keeps you from wasting time and costing you and your company money.

> **TALK TIP**
> For those customers who regularly don't call back, put them in your plan on different days or different times of the day to increase the likelihood of reaching them.

PRIORITIZE YOUR CALLS

To get your day off to a good start, begin with an easy call—a friendly, low-stress, positive situation. For example, a good first call might be an upbeat thank-you to a regular customer. Or it could be to a customer who is expecting a returned call regarding an inquiry. This type of call should yield a positive response and get your day started on a positive note.

After you decide what your first call of the day will be and the reasoning behind it, you need to prioritize the rest of the day's phone contacts. Here's how:

Priority 1: Scheduled appointments, as well as customers with the most potential to buy (not necessarily those who have bought the most in the past, but those who can give you the most business *in the future*).

Priority 2: Key decision makers who tend to be in their offices at certain times—for example, executives often get to their offices early in the morning before the business chaos begins.

Make your Priority 2 calls early. Call at 7:00 or 7:30 in the morning. Businesspeople are fresher, more alert, and less distracted at the start of the day than they are later, when more has occurred. Someone who is difficult to reach or who puts you off in the afternoon may be more accessible in a morning call.

Priority 3: Time zone–dictated calls. For example, in the Midwest and South most people leave for lunch between 11:30 and noon. In the Northeast, customers typically go to lunch around 1:00. And of course, people on the West Coast may be strolling back from lunch just when you are wishing you could call it a day. Consider calling a decision maker right before lunch. An alternative is to call *during* lunch when the assistant is out. Sometimes customers will even answer their own phone while eating a sandwich at their desk. This sort of call needs to be short and efficient, perhaps intended just to schedule another time to talk. You might also want to intentionally catch a decision maker's assistant during the lunch hour. That way, you can spend some time picking her brain.

To avoid missing customers at their very best time of the day, consider staggering your workday schedules—begin early some days, work later other days. Sometimes, if you are ahead of their time zone, calling your customers before everyone else gets started reduces your competition.

Also, ignore your colleagues who whine, "My customers don't work on Fridays." This is never true 100 percent of the time. It's just a flimsy excuse not to work on Fridays. For instance, many dentists don't work on Fridays, but mine does. Somebody, somewhere, is working on Friday; you can count on it. For the decision makers who travel a great deal, Fridays are often the only day they are likely to be in the office. Think of calling hard-to-reach customers at a time that is not routine for you, at a time that is not obvious—especially to your competition!

The final step in prioritizing your call time is to commit to beginning calls at a specified time. Be very focused about when your call day begins. If you plan to begin at 8 A.M., then make sure you are pressing buttons on your phone at 8:00. If it's a late-start/late-end day to accommodate different clients' schedules, then close out your eBay summary page by 10:30 in order to be ready to rock by your 11 A.M. start time. Just as schools have bells to signal the start of classes, you need to incorporate some sort of formal transition trigger for the opening of the business day—regardless of what time it is.

> **TALK TIP**
> Make a few calls *before* you get your coffee, *before* you check your email, and *before* you go to your eBay sale page. You'll be amazed at how much more productive each day is.

Launch Your Call Day

Though you will pace yourself through the day (according to your plan, of course), launching the workday instead of just oozing into it is important for your success to play out.

Make the decision the moment you wake up that you are going to have a profitable day. When you are ready to call, sit tall at your clutter-free desk and tell yourself, "Today I'm going to meet my goals." Be very specific about those goals. "Today I am going to make ninety calls." "Today I am going to close five customers." Your brain's expectations are powerful guides.

If you tell yourself that you will complete all your planned appointments (and believe it!), then your whole focus will be on accomplishment. One note for this mental preparation is to remind yourself that there are no such things as prospects; *they're all customers.* Now, say aloud, right here, as you read this:

THERE ARE NO PROSPECTS;

THEY ARE ALL CUSTOMERS

Success with a "prospect" is somewhat iffy, subject to all sorts of conditions. And customers will hear that iffyness in your voice over the phone. Success with a "customer" is a done deal. You've already closed him or her in your mind, so the rest is just working up to that end! Calling prospects creates a "might" or "could" expectation.

Have you ever heard the advice that says, "Don't think, don't try, just *do*"? Everyone is a customer, a "do," not a "prospect," or a "try." Positive self-talk will convince you that everyone will *become* your customer as a result of a conversation with you. And since you are on the phone, and not looking the customer in the eye, it will be easy for you to picture him or her saying, "Yes!"

This mindset will make your calls more successful.

> **TALK TIP**
>
> If you have chosen a thank-you for your first call, don't forget to ask for more business or a referral while you have this customer on the line; it's still a sales call. Using this tactic at the beginning will set you up for a successful day.

Your attitude is good, so you are feeling confident, in control, and ready to close more sales! Then, if you have some disappointing calls later, they are just a drop in the bucket.

Keep in mind that where you place your expectations is critical for achieving what you want. Expecting positive outcomes frees your brain for creative thought and strategizing. Constantly trying to protect yourself from possible negative outcomes can paralyze you. In addition, your customers can feel fear or hesitation over the phone. When they hear a lack of confidence, they have an even greater opportunity to shut you down instead of becoming engaged in conversation.

Open Calls with Confidence

Okay, your desk is clear, your notepad or whiteboard is ready, and your call day is under way. Before each call you make, remember to take fifteen seconds to determine your goal and your approach, and create an engaging opening statement. Here are some call opening ideas:

- The thank-you
- The referral
- The prospecting call
- The appointment confirmation call

THANK-YOU CALLS

A lot of people are calling your customers to sell products, but very few of them are thanking their customers for their business. Thank-yous seem to be falling out of our interactions altogether these days. For this reason, if for no other, you should offer appreciation to distinguish yourself from your competitors. Your customer may show his or her gratitude for the affirmation with a purchase order or a referral.

For an existing customer, the best opener might well be a thank-you, like both of the following examples:

"Ms. Johnson, this is Aaron Doe from XYZ Company. I want to thank you for your recent order."

"Mr. Levine, I understand you have been purchasing from our company for five years, and I want to thank you."

This will disarm most customers because they aren't used to getting such a call for their business. Sometimes you will want to "thank and run" to cement a good impression in the customer's mind. However, if the customer is responsive and jumps in to discuss business, or happens to mention being pleased with your product or service, then move forward. The dance is always driven by the customer. Let him or her call the shots.

REFERRAL CALLS

These are those social networking gems. Any time you can mention someone's name, you create a "virtual" introduction. You have something in common: you both know the person whose name you used for the referral. A call suggested by a respected colleague demands attention. At the very least you have, in a way, been introduced by the person who gave you the customer's contact information. While it's up to you to make the call work, you certainly are a step ahead in the customer's mind. If this is a referral call generated by a customer, an internal contact, a friend, or through networking, begin your call using the referral name. Your call might sound like this:

> "Robert, hello, this is Alex from PDQ Company. Mac Mac-Donald suggested I call you about your interest in stream-lining your purchasing."

PROSPECTING CALLS

This call is made to someone that neither you nor your company has a prior relationship with. Since prospectors look for gold, we can think of these calls in the same way. Someone whom you call will ultimately become a new customer because of your effort. So, depending on the value of an individual sale in your industry, it could be worth gold to you!

Of course we'd like every call to be an easy path, but sometimes you just have to use a machete to get through the jungle in order to reach the hidden riches. Most of us who make our living on the phone don't work for companies that have a staff of qualifying clerks to furnish us with prescreened contacts. For this reason we have to map our own way. So, load up with some good tools, like the examples below.

In a strong prospecting call, your opener should include a reference to something noteworthy about the customer's company or industry. For example, it might sound like this:

> "Ms. Denos, this is Maria Villalon from Aztec Pipefitting. I read in this week's *Wall Street Journal* that your company is preparing a rollout of three new locations. I'd like to speak with you regarding how we can assist you with your steel fabrication."

Remember that most people enjoy talking about themselves or their company, especially if there is something particularly good to be proud of.

Monitor your local business news publication (most larger cities have these), the business section of your local paper, or an online news source. Look for any changes in management, new product announcements, or contract awards. Sending a copy of the article with a note can be an excellent reason to call as a follow-up. The more you demonstrate what you already know about the company, the more your suggestions will sound like helpful information from a concerned source.

A certain part of your job is knowing what's going on in your customers' industries. When you know the business, the competitors, and the news, it will be easy for you to come up with the appropriate opening benefit statement. Another possible opener might be:

> "Ms. Denos, this is Angie Chin from Change Systems. Your company recently acquired XYZ, and I'm calling to discuss how we can save you time during the transition."

Even small companies have a presence on the Web these days. There's no reason why you can't find a reason to call or a pertinent item to discuss. That information will allow you to gain attention immediately and establish credibility quickly.

Notice that we didn't use that old word, "rapport." Schmoozing for personal rapport is a part of face-to-face conversation; it is a personal connection punctuated by body language and facial expression. Phone selling doesn't include those elements, so you are going to have to establish *value* for the time the customer allots for the call. Customers today are willing to trade you time for solutions or additions to their bottom line. They are not willing, however, to have their busy day interrupted to answer questions like, "How are you doing today?"

For anyone moving to inside sales, this is a shift of strategy. Forget the boring and inane intro that truly does nothing to connect you to the customer. You must show that you know the business challenges, that you are up to date on the industry, or even that you know the particulars of the company itself. This immediately sets you up as a possible partner in the customer's decision making. It also sounds a little more professional.

APPOINTMENT CONFIRMATION CALLS

Some of your calls for the day will be to confirm appointments that you have already set.

When calling to confirm an appointment, whether it's a phone or face-to-face appointment, here's a surefire way to keep from having your appointment canceled. Customers may want to cancel at the last minute because salespeople are not a priority in their work lives. Interruptions or disasters can occur, and priorities change between the time you secured the appointment and the appointment itself. So, always confirm call appointments by using voice mail. An enthusiastic reminder on a customer's voice mail gives them a nudge, but won't provide an easy opportunity to cancel your appointment. For example, call when you expect the customer to be out and leave the following message:

> "Hello, Michael, I'm looking forward to speaking with you at 3:30 today about an efficient way of solving your shipping problems."

But be wary. If you have to confirm the appointment when Michael might be in his office, call the main switchboard instead of his direct number. When you get the receptionist, ask to be forwarded to his voice mail, not his extension, and don't leave your number. If Michael doesn't have your number handy (and he probably doesn't), he won't call you to cancel. This holds true whenever you are making a confirmation call: Never leave your phone number.

TALK TIP

If you've been using email to confirm call appointments, you might want to rethink that practice. That reply button makes it too easy for customers to beg off. Their enthusiasm level is not the same now as it was when you scheduled the call, and without that initial enthusiasm, they might believe they're too busy to talk to you. In addition, although email may be your preferred communication medium, your customer may avoid it. Thus, a confirmation may go unnoticed. Lastly, with filled mailboxes and downed servers, email is just plain unreliable.

The Payoff

Everyone likes a sure thing. However, success is never a sure thing. This realization sometimes makes telephone salespeople hesitate or procrastinate when it is time to begin calling. The skills you have gained in this chapter will improve the odds of success, without doubt—*if you use them!* Planning, setting appointments, and ensuring your customers are available and "up for" your call appointments will improve your contact rate and, ultimately, your close rate and income.

The theme of this book is to S-T-A-R-T—in other words, get your ass on the phone! Start using some new tactics, start prospecting daily, start calling early, start leaving compelling messages—well, you get the idea. "Start" is more than a word to get you going: it's a very handy acronym to keep you on target. Use it to help you start making more money!

S — *SET UP* for success.

T — *TAKE CONTROL* of your call.

A — *ASK* high-value questions.

R — *REMOVE* all obstacles and close.

T — *TAKE CARE* of your customer.

Now that Linda's had the chance to look at the material in this chapter, let's see where she's going with her new prep plans and call openers:

"I understand your company just acquired XYZ Industries."

"The *Wall Street Journal* just reported that you are stream-lining your production and I'd like to ask you a question about that."

"Alex Janov said that we need to connect regarding your department's recent growth. I'd like to learn more."

Wow! Linda's got something legitimate to talk about with the very busy person on the other end of the line and she's much more likely to invite a conversation. If the customer is talking, Linda is selling. Okay you, start selling!

CHAPTER 2

Managing Time and Information for Profitability

PHONE SALES CHALLENGE – *Anthony, in IT placement, tells us: "I called a customer earlier today and was actually surprised when he answered the phone. Then I tried to find my notes from our previous conversation and they had disappeared!"*

Too often, sales pros get lost in thinking they don't have time to dig around for or keep track of details on customers. The focus is the phone call, the moment, right? Not even close! Today's customer doesn't have time for glib conversation. Unless you can offer something directly relevant to the customer's challenges in the very first breath, you are revealing that you're just another nuisance call. You might even be experiencing exchanges like these:

SALESPERSON: Oh, hi John, how are you today? This is Anthony, uhm, from xyz Services. I wanted to check with you to see, uh . . .

CUSTOMER (interrupting): Well, Anthony, I really don't have time to talk to you. Goodbye.

In this example Anthony clearly wasn't prepared for the call. He has forgotten that call-to-close ratios can be improved with solid customer information and call planning.

> **SALESPERSON:** Hi, Rebecca, I'm from ABC Enterprises. I'm not sure if I talked with you before or not, but I wanted to share an idea with you.

> **CUSTOMER:** Well, I'm sure that we haven't spoken before, and I can tell you that we have no interest. Goodbye.

Here's a typical example where a phone salesperson is excitedly promoting a new product or service. But since the salesperson isn't even organized enough to know if he or she has spoken with the customer before, the customer pretty quickly assumes that the call will be lame.

> **SALESPERSON:** This is Josh from Aggregate. I apologize because I know I was supposed to send you a confirmation email after our last conversation.

> **CUSTOMER:** I'm glad you called, but we had to make a decision last Tuesday. We really liked your product, but when we didn't hear from you . . .

Wow! Because of a lack of promised follow-up, this rep was blindsided by a major change in customer circumstances. If he was counting on this sale in his weekly report, he's certainly going to come up short. Commitments made to customers are tests of credibility. If you say you are going to follow up on Thursday, *do it*!

If you are a professional salesperson, and especially if you are on commission, time spent on the phone translates directly into money. But if that time is inefficiently or ineffectively spent, it will ultimately cost you. For this reason, maximizing the use of your time requires careful preparation for phone sales calls. This process includes locating contacts, tracking customer needs and accounts, and even enhancing your skills (such as reading this book). Improving your call-to-close ratios will pay off in large dividends.

First, you need to get a clearer picture of what your time is worth, and how to increase your dollar yield per hour, minute, and year.

Keep a consistent pattern of planning, tracking, and following up. If you fall down in any one of these areas, you're likely to become just another statistic of a failure caused by the inability to plan. This chapter is about making and improving that connection by managing your accounts and then gathering and utilizing customer information so that your call planning leads you to closing more sales. Information isn't just power—it's money!

Second, you need to improve your efficiency, both in finding qualified customers so that your phone time is well spent and in gathering and managing the information that is most useful to you in planning whom to call, how often to call, and even what time of day is best. The information storage system that you use can be customized for your purposes, but there is one absolute for successful phone selling: You must have sufficient information about the customer to establish credibility instantly. Your good looks and charm are not helpful when the customer can't see you.

Improve Your Time-to-Sales Ratio

There are many ways to increase your efficiency as a sales professional. None, however, are magical—nor will they work if you don't use them. The recommendations in this chapter might be a significant departure from "I've always done it that way." One truth emerges, however: If you continue your phone selling in the same way, you will get the same results.

Time management to increase your call-to-dollars relationship will require some changes on your part. Though many reasons exist for you to make some of these important changes, the best is the table in Figure 2-1.

THE TIME/COST TRADE-OFF

What is your time worth?

Let's break down the numbers to help determine why it's so important to improve your efficiency. As you look at this table, first figure out how much each hour of your time contributes to your income. Find your salary, then scan across to the column that tells you how much more green you can bring home by becoming more efficient—by eliminating wasted time, thus adding an extra hour to your working day.

Figure 2–1

How Much CAN You Make?

Annual Income	One hour is worth	One minute is worth	One extra hour/day adds
$50,000	$25.61	$0.43	$6,250/yr
$75,000	$38.42	$0.64	$9,375/yr
$100,000	$51.23	$0.85	$12,500/yr
$125,000	$65.10	$1.09	$15,884/yr
$150,000	$76.84	$1.28	$18,750/yr
$175,000	$89.65	$1.49	$21,875/yr
$200,000	$102.46	$1.71	$25,000/yr
$250,000	$128.07	$2.13	$31,250/yr
$300,000	$153.69	$2.56	$37,500/yr

©SalesPEAK, Inc., all rights reserved, www.salespeak.com.

If you waste an hour a day, look how much you have squandered. If you are on a commission plan, the numbers are even more dramatic. So, the way you manage your time has a direct impact on your income. If you are on straight commission, or receive bonuses, that extra hour each day you might spend shopping online sucks up more than cash. Wasted time translates directly into lost money for you.

Now, let's look at your day and see just where your time is spent. Do the following to help you understand more clearly where your time goes:

1. Track everything you do for three days, rounding your activity to fifteen-minute increments. From the first minute you pick up the phone, record what you do all day. Be honest with yourself, because no one will see this but you, and its purpose is to help you make more money through greater efficiency.

Note what wastes your time during the course of the day. Most people find that personal phone calls, chats at the coffee bar, and online activities are their worst enemies when it comes to time away from the phone.

2. At the end of the three days, sit in a quiet room and carefully analyze the log you've created to see how you are using your time. Take a look at what you, personally, have control over.

   Then consider how you can make better use of your time in different ways. After tracking your time, you might determine that by simply beginning your calls fifteen minutes earlier, which allows you to make eight more calls per day or forty more per week, you might close three more sales per week. If an average sale for you is $1,000, that adds up to $3,000 per week, which multiplied by fifty-two weeks equals an increase of $156,000 in sales per year!

   At a 10 percent commission rate, you have now generated an additional $15,600 by simply beginning fifteen minutes earlier each day. This seems like a small price to pay for a sizable return.

As soon as you seriously examine what you do with your time, you'll begin to see how much money you are losing to time-suckers. Although each person is different, every sales professional can manage time more effectively by choosing activities that enhance well-being, whether personal or professional. Taking care of your health, for example, by exercising, taking breaks, and getting out for lunch, is not wasted time: These activities result in better productivity. But if your friend doesn't like her job and she calls you to talk for an hour a day, she's costing you money.

At some point, you need to seriously weigh how much you need to make versus how much your time means to you—in actual dollars. Start thinking about concrete ways to optimize your selling time and invest your time wisely. Don't let it just pass by while you sip lattes and text your friends.

DISPELLING THE 80/20 RULE OF SALES

Every salesperson has heard of the 80/20 rule, that 80 percent of our business typically comes from 20 percent of our customers. It's amazing that we all seem to believe that this 80/20 rule exists no matter what our business is. Let this be the place where you finally hear that it may not be true.

The 80/20 rule presupposes a mathematical relationship. If your sales goal is predicated on 20 percent of your customers' business bringing in 80 percent of your sales, you are in danger of never making your goal. We cannot depend on history to determine our success because we live in a fluid world. Regardless of your industry, business constantly changes. Your best customer today may be acquired, merged, or go out of business, and your lowest revenue customer might expand. You could be blindsided by an unexpected turn of events and you will have absolutely no control over your ability to capitalize on the changes.

Your company may be rolling out a new product to a potential new market and you may find that you have no sales history with that type of customer. Perhaps these new customers will be the ones that will contribute the most to your growth. Your sales history is irrelevant. Future success should be your focus. This is especially true because the money from past sales is gone—either spent or absorbed. The only meaningful question for you as you prioritize your selling time must be, "What am I going to do *this* year?" Have you had a major customer that has gone out of business? What prime, top-of-the-line customer this year is one you couldn't even get on the phone last year? Begin analyzing your accounts to look for future business without presupposing the 80/20 classic rule.

PRIORITIZING CUSTOMERS

To determine how you are going to invest your time for maximizing sales, you'll need an *A, B,* and *C* customer identification matrix. Figure 2-2, Strategic Master Planning Form, shows a method of future account prioritizing that you might not have used in the past.

Figure 2–2

STRATEGIC MASTER PLANNING FORM

Name: _____   Territory: _____   Year: _____

Value 1–5 (low to high)

Account Name	Cust.	Compet.	Relat.	Size	Maint.	Credit	Pot'l	Total	A, B, C
Example Account	5	1	4	4	4	4	5	27	A

Notes:
Existing Customer of ours = 5
Competition has business = 1, we have business = 5
Size is relative to territory
Maintenance = time spent with handling complaints 1 = high maintenance

Potential = relative to territory
Total = Maximum of 35 points
A, B, C is relative to territory

Remember: you may weight any of the columns if you want, just make sure to be consistent!

© Renee Walkup, SalesPEAK, Inc. 678-587-9911, www.salespeak.com. All Rights Reserved.

Before you begin your planning, you'll need to honestly consider where your best customer *potential* lies. By filling out the matrix in Figure 2-2 for each of your customers and prospects, you will discover where you should be investing your time to maximize your income.

Consider these ideas when planning:

- What is your relationship with the buyer? On a scale of 1 to 5, your relationship might be a 4. If you have all the customer's business, that's a 5.
- Future growth potential may be a 5.
- You can total different categories and begin to look at all accounts.
- Perhaps totals of 27 to 35 would be an *A* account, 19 to 26 would be a *B*, and 18 or fewer would be a *C*.

This is a time-management and time-investment determiner, because you will never get your time back. Remember: You're planning for sales *growth*.

Look at the future. Some former *A* accounts might be maxed out, but *B*s might be in a position for greater growth. One other determiner from a time-management decision is "How needy is that account?" If there are complexities, problems, or a high need for attention, it may actually be in your best interest to assign the account to an account manager or to customer service because it might be costing you money in terms of your *time*. Remember, you are basing all these business-planning decisions on greatest result for time invested.

These are business decisions. If you don't have the freedom to choose these courses of action, make a case for a change and take it to your manager. A $15-per-hour employee can maintain an account, whereas your $80-per-hour attention for a limited return might not be a good business decision. As a phone sales professional, you need to spend your time doing what you do best—selling on the phone, not maintaining already sold accounts that lack growth potential.

Let's look at an example of an inside computer salesperson who secures a $1 million sale to Garrison School District. The school district also needed a service contract worth another $300,000. The total sale for the current year was $1.3 million. This is an *A* account for this territory.

Now it's time to plan for the new fiscal year. The salesperson considers this customer an *A* account, then schedules the time in his calendar to work the account, say, one call a week. A close examination, however, shows that it is, disappointingly, now only a $100,000 per year service account—not a priority at all for this territory. In fact, this customer won't be eligible as an *A* account for another two years after the existing contract is up. This account has thus become a *B* or *C* customer. Calls from the salesperson to this customer for the current year should be strategically reduced and not disproportionately allocated by occurring once weekly.

What about you? Are you thinking past or future? Your company most probably bases goals on projected revenues—not past sales. So, take a look at your *A, B,* and *C* accounts. You'll probably find that some of your *B*s are your best *A*s for the upcoming sales year. You'll also probably find that some of your *A*s are now *C*s because of buying patterns. Take a look at your business and make these forecasting determinations. Just be honest when evaluating each customer.

Now that your priorities have been determined, you have to parcel out your forty phone hours very efficiently. Because Garrison School District (in our previous example) was an *A* account last year, too many salespeople would spend an *A* equivalent number of calls when the potential for *new* business just isn't there. The result is wasted time that should be spent selling more to existing accounts and developing new accounts.

For example, in a forty-hour week:

- *A* accounts should take up approximately twenty-five hours of time (which includes planning, calling, leaving messages, having conversations with gatekeepers, and preparing proposals).
- *B* accounts require ten hours.

- *C* accounts require only five hours. (Voice mail messages, email, and mailings can be used instead.)

Remember that prioritizing is based on this year's potential, not last year's performance!

IMPROVING EFFICIENCIES IN DAILY ACTIVITIES

With the million and one activities you do each day as you make your phone calls, there are probably just as many ways to become more efficient. Some salespeople swear by wireless headsets. Some believe that a pen writes faster than a pencil. Scheduling calls in your CRM (Customer Relationship Management) software or device the day before saves planning time in the mornings when you have the most potential to reach customers.

Here are a few hints that can help you improve your efficiency:

Monitor your personal calls. These calls not only interrupt your day for the duration of the call, they make even the most focused salesperson procrastinate about getting work accomplished. Set aside a slow time of your sales day to deal with your personal business. You will be amazed at how much more efficient you will become when you plan your days this way.

Turn the audible signals off. If your email inbox, PDA, or mobile phone is ringing, it is difficult to concentrate on your customer calls. You'll be interrupted and wondering who's calling, whether it's important, and more.

Maximize your efficiency by having anything you might need at your fingertips. You shouldn't have to sift through personal bills, magazines, or your lunch leftovers. Organizational experts say to put the other items away where they are not distractions or clutter.

Set time goals for yourself. "I will make twenty-five calls before ten o'clock" or "I will make forty calls by noon." At the end of the time, get up and reward yourself. Be sure to plan your reward in advance so you don't lose a lot of time figuring out what you would like to do. By stopping at the end of a goal time *and* returning to calling at the end of your break, you stay fresher and put more energy into your calls. Tired people dawdle. It's better to organize your day around calls than to call arbitrarily until you are too exhausted to pay attention.

Clear your desk at the end of every day. Things that become covered on your desk rarely receive proper follow-up. Hunting for misplaced reports, notes, or orders is time-consuming. Reduce your paper by recording your call information regularly into your electronic tracking system.

Once you have begun managing your time by cutting out time-suckers and by efficiently organizing your phone call preparation, you will need to develop a solid system for locating and tracking customers.

Locate Quality Customers

One activity that does not differ whether you are selling in person or selling by phone is uncovering leads that can point you in the direction of quality customers. Leads are the lifeblood of your selling process and finding them is where your selling begins.

EXTERNAL RESEARCH

Here are some sources of likely leads for your sales calls:

- Existing customers—clients who are purchasing regularly.
- Inactive customers—clients who have bought before but not lately.
- Potentials—people in your database who have been contacted either by you or a predecessor but have not yet bought.
- Passive leads—leads generated by an inbound call to your company from a website registration, trade show, interest card from a magazine or advertisement, letter of inquiry, or a coupon.

- Referrals—leads generated by customers, employees, acquaintances, organization members, or other potentials.
- Networking—involvement in associations, groups, or face-to-face types of activities, including alumni organizations, chambers of commerce, volunteer organizations, industry groups, training, or speaker events.
- Industry publications—magazines, newspapers, local business publications, or online sources.
- Lists purchased from third-party sources—these can be defined by target market parameters.
- Suppliers and business partners—people who sell in the same industry but are not competitors.
- Web searches—keywords, industry articles, and similar searches.

> **TALK TIP**
>
> Going into a search engine to explore conferences and trade shows in your industry can be time well spent, because having a name to call on the phone helps you to navigate around any gatekeepers. Using a search engine can make it easier to find the specific names of presenters at conferences and booth personnel at trade shows. An added bonus is that it gives you something to immediately discuss with the prospective customer—their conference presentation or trade show experience!

Since we've just mentioned networking, let's look at a special category of networking sources, social networking sites. Every investigator and military officer knows the value of "recon" (reconnaissance). Any information about a customer gives you inside knowledge that you can use for strategizing. The Internet offers many organized sources for this information in the form of networking sites such as LinkedIn, MySpace, and Facebook.

LinkedIn specifically has a question, "What are you working on?" Everyone on your network list can see and comment on that. If you know someone who has access to an entry, then you can follow through on it as well. You can also invite contacts to LinkedIn. If they accept your invitation, you can get access to customer updates and use that information to keep your callbacks current. In addition, you will know if some new contract or expansion is coming.

For either a potential or existing customer you can find out what's new: travel, new contracts, etc. Go to that decision maker's page or, better yet, pinpoint a specific product (or service) that might connect directly with what he or she is doing. Sure this takes more time, but is this customer a significant growth opportunity for you? Could this be a potential top-ten account? It might be worth that extra five or ten minutes to add personal information to your database about an important decision maker or a large account.

For example, in a conference call about a proposal a sales rep noticed a casual comment about an art project the customer was working on. A visit to one of the social networking websites revealed that this person was not only a decision maker with the company but an artist "on the side." When the rep later followed up on the proposal by phone, she was able to make direct reference to the website. She so impressed the decision maker with her knowledge that she gained an important foothold, which eventually led to a sale.

INTERNAL RESEARCH

Your company's intranet can tap you into forecasting programs, inventory pages, online slide presentations, and even your organization's customer service department. These are good places to get leads. If your customer service personnel or sales support teams are trained to address service situations as sales opportunities, access to those records or personnel can result in new business.

For example, recurrent technical problems could mean that a better or upgraded product would be appropriate. If a personal trainer has purchased home-use equipment and trains many clients all day on the equipment, he or she might be having problems with it, since it wasn't designed for such heavy use. For you, the salesperson, this knowledge gained from customer service might provide a valuable lead that could result in a sale of commercial-grade equipment.

Think about who else in your company has opportunities to uncover leads. For example, who are your customers' employees contacting within your organization? And what might your boss or predecessor know about a customer? Perhaps one of your business partners or vendors knows about a customer's situation. Trade show exhibitors and attendees are a valuable source of information for many salespeople as well. Of course, you'll want to check the prospect's website and use the Internet to obtain additional company information.

Just as important as uncovering leads is the need to break down those leads according to their potential. This helps you prepare a blueprint to guide your sales calls. Phone time ROI (return on investment) relates directly to the revenue potential of the individual or organization on the other end of the phone. Plan your day around gaining new accounts and be wary of spending too much time on accounts that perhaps just bought but won't be up for additional purchases again soon, like the Garrison School District.

Now that you've explored these important sources of client acquisition, let's look at what data you should be gathering and storing on these potential customers.

Gather and Manage Customer Information

You need to keep track of a great deal of information about your customers. Since everyone's company does this differently, this section will be a rough guideline for what kind of information you need to maintain and which methods work best to store that information for easy retrieval.

KEY ELEMENTS OF A CONTACT MANAGEMENT PROGRAM

Filling in a document (electronic or otherwise) similar to the form presented on the next page on each of your customers will keep their vital information in one place, available when you need it. No more wondering where that scrap of paper with the cell phone number went, no more wondering if you have their name spelled correctly, or their precise title for the memo you are writing.

Essential Information

Name: _____

Title: _____

Position: _____

Phone number and extension: _____

In addition to the essential information that's needed for easy retrieval, you'll want to include the following in your contact management program:

Cell or alternative phone: _____

Time zone: _____

Fax number: _____

Email address: _____

Physical address: _____

Company website URL: _____

Status designation (existing customer, prospect, referral, cold call, strategic partner, etc.): _____

Occasion of discovery (networking function, met on plane, etc.):
_____

Sales history: _____

Products/services used: _____

Customer since (year): _____

Service agreements (yes/no): _____

Renewals: _____

Lease expiration: _____

Follow-up date: _____

Assistant's name/phone: _____

Home phone: _____

Personal interests (sports, organizations, associations, etc.):

_____

Spouse name, children's names: _____

Referred by. _____

Personality type (see chapter 3): _____

Best times to reach:_____

Competitors (direct and indirect): _____   _____

Notes or comments (captured conversations, dates, discussions, etc.):

_____

_____

Link to a proposal or sales agreement, if applicable:

_____

_____

In addition to the data above, you might also include information such as how decisions are made and whether the customer contact person is a gatekeeper or purchasing agent, or whether this individual simply makes purchasing recommendations.

As you can see, the information that can be gathered on a customer from behind the scenes is practically limitless. You just need to decide what is important, with "more" often better. However, more information is useful only if you can catalog and retrieve it in a timely and purposeful way. The following approaches can help you manage the customer information you gather.

METHODS OF KEEPING CUSTOMER RECORDS

Now that you have strategically gathered a full range of "recon" on your customers, you will have to determine how best to manage it all. Information is just data; you will have to record it in some meaningful way using a medium that makes sense for your work style and company. Here are various methods of record keeping with the advantages and disadvantages of each.

Pen and Paper Methods. Pen and paper methods of keeping customer records can include using index cards, call report forms, or paper files.

The advantages are that these methods:

- Improve your ability to retain customer data.
- Create visual and hands-on organizational systems.
- Keep direct quotes or customer details private.

When you hold a pen or pencil and write down customer information such as interests and needs, you mentally retain it longer than you would otherwise. Neurological studies have shown that writing by hand is actually more effective for memory retention than keying in the data electronically. Then, when you transfer the information to your database, you reinforce the memory.

If you are a visual person, you can use a color system of files or index cards for cataloging—for instance, past customers could be pink, current large customers green, and so forth. For some people, having a physical, hands-on organization system is the most helpful.

The disadvantages of these methods of retaining customer information are that:

- Individual pieces get lost.
- Papers and cards must be filed.
- File cabinets take up space.
- Information may not be easily transferable to someone else who might need it, such as a sales manager, another rep, or your customer service department.
- Management of hard-copy information can be time consuming—collating, alphabetizing, filing.
- Paper records are heavy and bulky, especially where there are many customers.
- Too many possible problems (illegible handwriting, misplaced information, lack of space on a note card, etc.).

Electronic Methods. Electronic methods of keeping customer records can include using specialized software on your desktop or laptop and personal digital assistant (PDA). In addition, our cell phones are hand-sized information storage devices, although they are not always the easiest to use for planning purposes.

You may have a company database system adapted from existing software or created specifically for company use. Off-the-shelf products, including Web-based programs, work well, too.

An electronic management system can be as minimal or robust as you prefer. Since there is such a broad range of prices and applications, you should be aware of what you actually need. Readily available customer contact management software includes ACT!, GoldMine, and Salesforce.com. A recent search on Yahoo yielded thirty-five listings of CRM software, including some open-source offerings.

Many of these programs can be put onto company networks, so your information technology manager might need to be involved in your consideration of which to choose. You can also find software that is compatible with PDAs, but be sure to check for compatibility with your company's hardware and software systems.

The advantages of using electronic methods of record keeping are that:

- They are reliable.
- Portable devices are easy to use and connect with desktop systems quickly.
- Information is easily duplicated and backed up.
- Records can be kept for a long time to track purchasing history.
- Databases allow you to use many different identifiers to locate customers. For example, you might remember that a customer likes California wines and that you met the person at a telecom conference, but you can't remember the person's name. With a robust database, you'll be able to find that individual effortlessly.
- Data can be backed up regularly and easily to reduce the risk of lost information.

The disadvantages of using electronic methods are that:

- Desired software packages might be cost-prohibitive.
- Your IT department might restrict use or flexibility of the company system.
- You might not have the staff or time to convert data—transcription, scanning, etc.
- You could lose your PDA or handheld computer.
- A virus in your desktop computer or on your company's network could cause you to lose everything.

Whatever contact management software you choose, be sure it is flexible enough to allow you to create your own fields. One example might be "I.D." In this field, you could record how you know a customer. Perhaps you met this person at a conference, professional association meeting, school alumni party, or even at the gym or in a seminar. This field is also an ideal location to include a referral name so that when you call the customer, you can use the referral name.

Sometimes, as part of planning, you will contact everyone you met through a specific association or at a certain seminar. You can customize a phone or mail campaign based on an approach relevant to those people in a particular organization.

You can also sort by fields to plan. For example, you might decide that you want to plan your day by contacting customers in a particular time zone or zip code and, using your contact manager, you can call customers in those areas. Make sure that the system is robust enough to hold the tracking information you need—and, of course, be sure to fill it in: empty fields will not help you one bit. Also, choose a system that is easy to operate; otherwise, you won't use it.

You may inherit a system that your predecessor used or that your company dictates and find that it's not working for you. If that's the case, you may need to adjust (with approval) your planning and tracking system. Whatever you use, be consistent with your procedures—effective record keeping is essential to your sales success.

> ### A Greener Way to Do Business
>
> Planning and tracking by utilizing your preferred contact management system or CRM is a much greener method of record keeping than paper files, which use a substantial amount of carbon dioxide from processing paper.

The Payoff

Whatever method you use to make the most of your calling time, you are bound to be able to improve your efficiency. Far too many salespeople never even ask themselves if their work could be managed better or more economically. If you are getting the same numbers or, worse, higher quotas on shrinking territories, you will have to improve somewhere. Addressing the management of your professional activities to make your time work better for you is money in your pocket and time for living a balanced life.

Let's see what Anthony is saying now:

"I spent a half hour on Geek.com today and got three new leads from a news item, put them in my database, called them referencing their new expansion, and set up appointments with all three!

"Just last week I was heading out the door to a meeting when my CRM system alerted me of a follow-up that I was supposed to do with a new potential. So I called on my cell phone, and the customer said, 'Well, hello Anthony, I was expecting your call. Do you know that you're the only rep on this bid who has called back when he said he would? That's the kind of person I want to work with.'

"I got the business just by 'showing up' by phone on time. But I have to admit that I never would have remembered to make the call if I hadn't gotten the alert."

CHAPTER 3

Identifying Personality Types Over the Phone

PHONE SALES CHALLENGE – *Alesia, in equipment sales, had this to say: "You know how you just click with some people? I wish it were that way with all my customers. I could make a fortune."*

Ah, yes. How much easier it is to sell to someone who seems to be on the same wavelength that you are. Not only are these people easier customers to work with, but you often find that you genuinely like them. In that phone selling fantasy where every word you say clicks, you are the star revenue producer in your company. In real life, however, there are occasions where the person on the other end of the phone just doesn't seem to respond to what you're saying. Creating a conversation with this customer is arduous and seems practically impossible.

Look at what happens when personality and communication styles don't match:

CUSTOMER (answering the phone in a monotone voice): Hello, this is Jackson.

SALESPERSON (briskly, in a high-energy manner): I'm really excited that you contacted us, and we're rolling out this new product and . . . "

CUSTOMER: Who is this again? And what did you want?

Energy level, characterized by enthusiasm over the phone and speed of delivery, is one area of communication compatibility (or incompatibility). In the following example, the caller is explaining to the potential customer some important information that he felt would establish credibility for his company. The customer rushes him off the phone because he perceives that the conversation is taking too long to get to a point.

CUSTOMER (tersely): This is Fred.

SALESPERSON (in clear and measured tones): This is Benjamin Ahrenhauser from Alexander Environmental and Associates. We've been in the environmental conservation business since 1987 and this year we received the J. D. Power award of excellence for . . ."

CUSTOMER (interrupting): I don't really care about 1986, and I don't have time for this.

SALESPERSON: No, it's 1987.

CUSTOMER: What? (Hangs up.)

In the example that follows, the salesperson is pushing in a matter-of-fact way, but the person on the other end isn't comfortable with the role of decision maker and hands the caller off. This may or may not lead to another contact, but not likely today.

CUSTOMER (answering phone in a friendly and warm tone): Good afternoon, Parts Department, this is Janice, how can I help you today?

SALESPERSON (in a very direct and businesslike manner): This is Tony with XYZ. We met at that trade show in Sacramento and I wanted to know when you're going to place an order.

CUSTOMER (stammering a bit): Well, uh. Yes, I think I remember being at your booth, and as I recall I was with Landry and Neal. Uhm. This is really their department. Maybe I can get them to call you. It's great to hear from you; maybe call back later when I've talked with them.

All of these customers that the salespeople couldn't even start a conversation with are buying from someone, although most likely not them. Remember, you can't make a living closing business with only those people who vibrate at the same frequency you do. When you develop an understanding of the communication needs of various personality types, as well as natural matches and clashes with your own personality, you will be much more able to generate that connection with *all* customers.

How many expressions can you think of in today's conversations that validate the other person's statements or motivations? Let's look at a few:

- "I get what you're saying."
- "Yeah, I see where you're coming from."
- "Uh-huh, uh-huh, I'm following you."

The opposite situation, a speaker's desire to be understood, has created a language of its own:

- "Ya'see?"
- "Do you hear me?"
- "Are we on the same page here?"

Though a smile seems to be a universal way to make a connection with someone, you can't close a sale with just a smile. And, of course, it's even trickier to get that smile across over the phone.

Being in tune with your customers, however, is often the determining factor in making a sale. You will be able to hit it off with nearly all your customers when you use strategies that place you in harmony with their respective personalities. Harmony equals sales. Learning to get on the same frequency as each of your customers will dramatically increase your close rate. You may think that recognizing a customer's personality type may be more difficult over the telephone than in person, but there are definitely clues you can learn to identify.

Once you are accustomed to the process, identifying your customer's buying styles over the phone will become an easy exercise for you in just about every call.

Of course, it helps to understand what your own personality type is as well. This knowledge lets you capitalize on your strengths with some customers, and manage your natural incompatibilities with others. For this reason, you will find a quick assessment in Appendix A that will help you to determine your type.

To be the peak sales performer you can be, you will need to learn the following four categories into which your customers are likely to fall:

Precise
Energized
Assured
Kind

Remember, you can close each of these personality types, if you use the right strategies. You'll need to adjust specific elements of your presentation style many times a day as you talk with different personalities. This is not an easy task, as it takes both planning and attention, but the payoff means more dollars for you.

A Greener Way to Do Business

Since 1970, there has been more than a threefold increase in passengers flying throughout the United States. According to the Federal Aviation Administration, these numbers are expected to double by 2025. Use a PEAK process to gain a better understanding of your customer over the phone, and avoid those long delays, the wasted hours of travel, excessive air fares, and increased air pollution.   *Source: faa.gov*

The Precise Customer

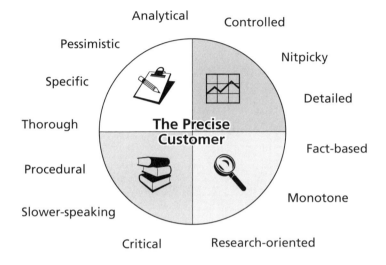

The **Precise Customer** needs to be correct and certain about decisions he or she makes and the implications of those decisions. Thus, they research and analyze carefully, and never make a decision based on just an impression or a gut feeling. Because they have to "get it right," they are careful, never impulsive. Always seeking more information and wanting to be absolutely certain, they will even risk a deadline in search of convincing proof. After your sales call, even if you are able to gain a tentative agreement, the **Precise Customer** will want to see a formal proposal. Under stress, **P**s will avoid you because, if they are undecided, a phone call or meeting feels like extra pressure from the salesperson.

These are the hardest customers to sell over the telephone. Even though you have overcome all the possible impediments to a close, they will likely still want time to think. The logical nature of facts and computers makes them more comfortable with data than with interpersonal situations. **Precise Customers** are task-oriented and generally very organized. In particular, they are likely to resent a phone interruption, so it is better to have an appointment for even a phone call for this customer.

Technical proficiency is a value to them, so fields such as engineering, computer hardware and software, science (especially research), accounting, and finance will include many people from the **Precise** category. Because of their expert knowledge, they are often consulted on decisions by higher-ups but will avoid making major decisions on the company's behalf. Over the phone, these customers may sound monotone, and you will hear this in their voice mail. It can be frustrating to deal with them because they will not reveal emotions, even if they are enthusiastic about your product.

These customers are proud of their own expertise and may be negative about the expertise of others. In character, however, they have a great deal of integrity, and although slow to make a decision, they can be counted on. These are the worker bees in their organizations and are often overworked and underappreciated.

STYLE-MATCHING STRATEGY FOR PHONE SUCCESS

To match a **Precise** buying style, you need to avoid too much enthusiasm in your communication patterns. Your phone style should be measured, deliberate, and controlled. **Precise Customers** think before they speak (unlike many of us in sales who think *by* speaking). For this reason, it may be common for them to be silent for a time after you ask a question—possibly long enough to make you uncomfortable. The **P Customer** requires extra time to process information. It's not an intelligence issue but a processing one.

While **Precise Customers** can be difficult to deal with on the telephone, they are by no means impossible. Be sure to give **P**s time to digest information; **P**s are not reactive thinkers. For example, you and your customer may be viewing a PowerPoint or information page on the company's website during a call. A classic error salespeople commit with **P**s is not allowing them time to read and study what is there. Huge mistake! If you have been successful in getting **P**s to your site (and you may get only one shot at this), they may sell themselves if allowed to fully explore the information there. Be quiet and let these customers look at the material on the website. Silence on the other end of the phone is not necessarily a bad thing with a **P**.

Since you are giving **P**s a lot of information, be sure to organize it for easy access. As the expert, **P**s will not go to bat for you or your product in decision meetings, unless there is plenty of documentation to substantiate the recommendation. (*Note*: This "once removed" situation, where someone will be your spokesperson with a decision maker, is not uncommon in phone selling, especially with **P**s, since they are respected by others.) **P**s will not take the risk of losing expert status by expressing enthusiasm over a product they can't back up.

If you are a different personality type from them, s-l-o-w down in all aspects of your phone conversation and be prepared to match their deliberate and thoughtful pace. Temper your own enthusiasm and any behavior that would rush a close or try to pin these customers down. Also, have the relevant facts and figures at your fingertips before calling **Precise Customers**. Answer all questions as completely as possible. If you don't have an immediate answer, call back with the answer as soon as possible.

Avoid generalities and testimonials, unless you have one from someone the **Precise Customer** knows and respects. And along this same line, be prepared to send proof in the form of documentation and articles from third-party sources (not press releases from your own company, but articles from industry magazines or tests by independent groups). A **P** won't necessarily take your word for it over the phone.

Use a careful and strategic sales approach—it works great with this group—and follow up often with regular contact, especially if you have new information or "hard" evidence of your product's superiority. Be certain to check for errors in anything you plan to say to them over the phone. You can bet that the **Precise Customer** is writing your facts down or logging the data into a PDA or laptop and will check your figures after you have hung up!

APPROACHES TO USE WITH THE PRECISE CUSTOMER

Remember: You are on the phone and body language is out as a communicator, so your words take on more value. Make your presentation at a slower pace; control your enthusiasm. Communicate what the **Precise Customer** needs to hear to enable him or her to come to a decision in your favor. These can include:

- References to white papers or third-party research.
- Reviews in major industry or educational publications or e-zines.
- Test results and data tables—*hard proof.*
- Documentable facts (and the **Precise** will want the source).
- Operations details.
- Risk assessments.
- Engineering principles behind your process or product.
- Specifications, materials, performance parameters.
- Concrete operational or design benefits.

The Energized Customer

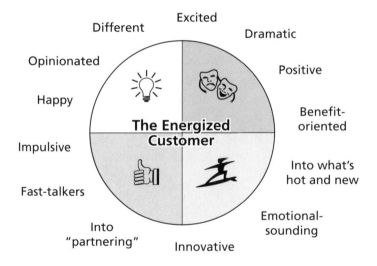

The **Energized Customer** will help you get your energy level back up if you're fading because they're infectious with optimism. Friendly, but hurried, they will talk fast and a lot. Using colorful words, they like to tell you about themselves and their projects, so they're not the best listeners. (Oops! Could this be you as a salesperson? How are *your* listening skills?) Es are assertive and may even sell themselves on your product as they explore possibilities. Just remember to be quiet and let this type of customer talk!

Even at their fast pace, the **Energized Customer** is a poor time manager and tends to be disorganized. You should assume they will lose documents you send; be prepared with backup copies. They also are not likely to take notes of your phone conversation and might forget important points. Because these customers respond well to people they like and can be impulsive as decision makers, you can profit from this scenario if you cultivate their friendship. But if they get mad at you, you will lose their business.

You will probably be calling more frequently with **Energized Customers**, because they will want to build a relationship before they do business with you. Because Es are persuasive and opinionated by nature, they will typically provide you with referral business. You'll just need to ask!

STYLE-MATCHING STRATEGY FOR PHONE SUCCESS

Energized Customers will respond to your requests for favors, "Will you just take some time to look at something for me? I'd appreciate your judgment and comments." Pay them compliments, as they like fueling their positive inclinations. These customers might not have a referral's phone number handy, but they would probably consent to a conference call and give a testimonial, if you ask (as long as they don't have to do anything to set it up!). Remember, though, that under stress, if things go wrong they will blame outside forces because they really see things as not their fault.

If your company has small promotional gifts you can send to the **Energized Customer**, these will be appreciated, as would any kind of personal remembrance. An example would be: "I remember you said your son played basketball. The PR department sent me a Knicks T-shirt and I thought he might like it, so I'm sending it out in tomorrow's mail."

Send them brochures and customize materials and presentations as much as possible; use color (and remember, you may have to send them a second time). Emails should be friendly and with bullet points. Stress the benefits to an **E** personally of using your service. Be sure your voice is upbeat and enthusiastic over the phone. Use more inflection and speak a bit faster—it may sound a bit exaggerated, especially if you're not the same personality type—but remember that the phone dilutes the effect of your vocal variety.

Emphasize the relationship by telling them how important their business is to *you*. Convey the notion of team: Their success and yours are tied together. You'll want to get a commitment from them before you get off the phone. Since **Es** are notoriously disorganized, setting up a deadline or a date and time will help you move forward in your next steps with these buyers.

An added tip: Remember to use thank-yous often with an **E Customer**. Sometimes a phone call just to thank an **E** for business is a great relationship builder. A handwritten follow-up note is another good idea.

APPROACHES TO USE WITH THE ENERGIZED CUSTOMER

Communicate what the **Energized Customer** needs to hear:

- Excitement in your voice over your product.
- Upbeat attitude, faster tempo of presentation.
- "Congratulations! You made a great selection!"
- New or innovative aspects of your product or service.
- Referrals from others who have bought from you.
- "This is an easy implementation since you already have your funds."
- Phone calls that are fun and interesting.
- Recognition and requests for the **E**'s opinion.

The Assured Customer

Assertive and focused, the **Assured Customer** is all business. Although very opinionated, they are clear on what they like and don't like, and so are very decisive. They will innovate and experiment, as it supports their vision. **Assureds** are committed to their goals and will go along with products/services that support those goals; however, they tend *not* to be loyal to individual sales reps or suppliers.

Strong leaders themselves, they respect those who have passed their tests and proven themselves worthy. One absolutely necessary element in every call to an **A** is reconnaissance—you must know the company and the **A**'s strategic needs. And there will be a test; in fact, every conversation can make or break the close.

Assured Customers may not return calls, just to see if you have pluck enough to pursue them, or they might sound abrupt in a way that would scare away the fainthearted. They use the distance of the phone to their advantage. But to the victor go the spoils with this one, because they are often major decision makers and have the potential to be your best customers.

Assureds may value time or efficiency over money, so be wary of using the dollars-off approach—which may work with many of your other customers—as a "sure" strategy. Because they are so time-conscious, if they suspect you will waste their time, they will cut you off. They aren't rude, per se; they're just serious about doing business, not engaging in chitchat. For this reason they avoid details, and so will want the short version or "executive summary." On the other hand, if you can handle with a succinct phone call what others want to do in person or in a rambling conversation, you will be able to get through when the competition cannot.

STYLE-MATCHING STRATEGY FOR PHONE SUCCESS

Know their vision! **Assureds** make their decisions based on where they want to go and what will help them get there, so they are quick to make a decision and then move on. Be fast and well prepared and don't waste time with "How are you?" and "Did you have a good weekend?" or any extraneous information. If you ask for ten minutes, note when ten minutes are up and offer to get off the phone. Your call plan should use the "three bullet" method. Think of the three items you want to cover, and be prepared to move quickly through the call.

Always sound confident as you demonstrate direct benefits quickly. You can play to the ego of the **Assured** by connecting your product/service directly to their main goal.

Finally, expect that they are multitasking while on the line with you, so be prepared to reel them in occasionally or to do a quick feedback check to ensure they are still with you on the phone. However, these are the customers who are most eager to conduct business with the most persistent callers. So, call early and call often to get an **A**'s attention.

APPROACHES TO USE WITH THE ASSURED CUSTOMER

Communicate what the **Assured** needs to hear:

- Respect for their time: "Charlie, do you have a quick five minutes?" (they'll be more likely to take your calls).

- "I'll call you back on Monday." These are busy people who no-toriously do not return calls and will expect you to call them.
- Brief voice mail messages delivered at a quicker pace.
- Direct and assertive phrasing. Avoid fawning or obsequious language like "please" or "I'd like to."
- Focus on speed of execution: "We can wrap this up with one call." You may get the deal because you act more quickly.
- "This will have direct bottom-line impact." Everyone likes to hear this, but **Assureds** more than anyone.

> **TALK TIP**
> Use power words such as "opportunity," "important," "your goals," "timesaving," and "competitive." And throw around (correctly, of course) managerial terms like "return on invest-ment," "supports strategic initiatives," "meeting objectives," and "eliminating waste spending."

The Kind Customer

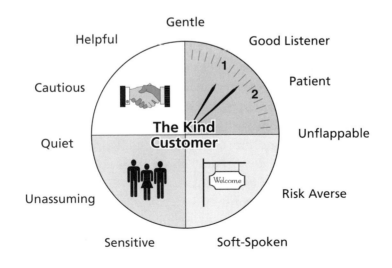

Warm, compassionate, and people-oriented, **Kind Customers** are good listeners and often a relief to talk to after some of the tougher types. They typically will take calls readily since they are people-pleasers. They are unhurried and patient over the phone, never seeming to be rattled—even if they *are* under stress. However, be aware that these are sometimes your most challenging customers since they are so slow to make decisions.

Kind Customers are loyal and will often stay with you, but they are *very* difficult to "steal" from their current supplier; **K**s don't like change. **Kinds** will be warm, considerate, and agreeable, even if they are not going to buy from you. This can be deceptive. There can be cultural implications here, also, as some cultures feel it is disrespectful to be impolite or unkind to a person, whether there is any intent to actually do business or not.

Team decisions are more comfortable for this type, and **K**s will rarely go against the consensus. Under stress, you can probably get this person to say "yes" to give in, but "no" will be the real answer and you will get no follow-through. This customer needs time to make a decision that will stick in the long term. **Kinds** have often experienced being taken advantage of in the past, and this affects their ability to make quick decisions. It takes a long time to gain their trust.

STYLE-MATCHING STRATEGY FOR PHONE SUCCESS

Because of the desire to be nice to all parties involved, **Kind Customers** need to feel that you will help them with others in the decision-making team. Recognize that **K**s rarely make decisions alone. You will need to find out who the other players are, but, with the right kind of safe questioning, your **Kinds** will likely happily tell you. Be sure to tell them, "Take your time," in your most patient voice and *mean it.*

They will expect conversation, so ask these customers how their day is going and listen for the answer. Since your sales call is also a relationship-continuing conversation, you will want to refer to something they told you about themselves in a prior call (there are excellent databases to help you keep track of these little personal details).

Let them get to know you, personally, your company, etc. You will find them sincere in their interest; to them a product is the whole package—company, product, *and* you. Knowledge on all these fronts will lower the perceived risk for **Kind Customers**. Don't push your **K**s in your phone calls. They will give in under duress, but it will be a meaningless win on your part. They won't follow through, so the sale is lost.

APPROACHES TO USE WITH THE KIND CUSTOMER

To close the deal, communicate what the **Kind Customer** needs to hear:

- Friendly, nonthreatening approach.
- Softer tone—avoid stress or an edge in your voice.
- Gentle questions with options instead of pushy close.
- Patient manner that invites questions and clarification.
- Assurance that the decision is good for everyone.
- Risk is reduced because of partnership with you.
- Details are taken care of and problems are handled.

> **TALK TIP**
> Most customers' personalities are evident from their recorded phone message or their tone of voice when answering the phone. You can prepare for real conversations by listening to customers' voice mail recordings. An opportune way to do this and identify the personality style is to call after hours and just listen to their voice mail. This will help prepare you for when you make the real call.

Personality Matches and the Phone Salesperson

As a salesperson, you have your own style and your own personality, whether on the phone or in person. By taking the PEAK Personality Type Assessment in Appendix A, you can get a clearer picture of your own type. In addition, you will be able to profit from understanding how to adapt your style to be the most effective with other customer personalities, by voice and style alone.

Remember, in romance, opposites attract; but in our work life, we need harmony in order to do business effectively. Thus, we synchronize best with those who are most like us. When we meet our similar type, it's a beautiful world, especially when that similar type is our customer. We feel the harmony; we hit on the same notes, operate in the same rhythm. The phone line is almost a mental bridge between two minds.

Even when we meet our opposite, though, we can look for the elements we have in common. In the old days, phone salespeople were taught to get people to talk about their personal lives, so they could determine elements in common: sports, hobbies, kids, and so forth. Today's customers don't have time for such chitchat, but we can still establish the connection they require before they will do business with us. Instead of interests in common, we learn to pay attention to voice, style, energy, and inflection. Watch for the clues and choose your strategy accordingly. That's the quick way to the payoff.

The Phone Salesperson's Quick-Reference Extra: The Salesperson ↔ Customer Match

What follows is a guide for handling the different customer types, once you know your own. Have you taken the test in Appendix A to determine your own personality type yet? You'll find what follows much more useful if you have.

THE PRECISE SALESPERSON

If you are the **P** salesperson, when you are in a **P** ↔ **A** relationship, you have in common tasks and goals, and interest in the job done right.

For **P** ↔ **K**, neither you nor the customer makes rash decisions; both of you are passive and precise, and with good listening skills between you. Although for different reasons, you are both somewhat cautious.

Look out, though, for the **P** ↔ **E** potential train wreck; you are *opposites*. Although contrary to your nature, if you don't communicate energy and passion for your product or service, you will not connect with the **E. Es** talk faster and are more emotional than you might be comfortable with. Don't let their rapid speech and high excitement level put you off. Remember, also, that the **E** may close the sale quickly. Avoid the temptation to keep offering information and details; the **E** will lose interest, and you might lose the sale. Sometimes an **E** just "feels right" about a sale, and although this might be a foreign notion to you, relax and celebrate it as good news.

THE ENERGIZED SALESPERSON

In the **E** ↔ **A** combination, if you are an **E** and the customer is an **A**, the elements you have in common are:

- High energy.
- Aggressiveness.
- Lack of concern for details.

Members of the **E** ↔ **K** relationship also share certain characteristics:

- Liking people.
- Courtesy.
- Warmth.

The bad news comes for the **E** ↔ **P** situation. If you are an **E** and the customer is a **P**, you have nothing in common naturally. For this *opposite* situation, you must change your style entirely. Of course, this takes a lot of energy to do, and choosing to go this extra mile when the stakes are high separates the big money salespeople from the lesser ones.

Remember, most of us don't get to choose the customers we have to work with. Less successful salespeople spend most of their time with customers they like, whether those are the highest ticket customers or not. Beware of falling into this trap.

An example of this is a phone salesperson whose clients are in the dental profession. She and most of her sales team are either **E** or **A**. Almost all their customers are **P**. The team had to work harder to develop solid sales relationships with the dentists (their customers), but by adjusting presentation styles to fit the customer, they closed dramatically more sales.

It is very easy to feel good about a customer who spends money with you. So, the extra work needed to adjust and perform more strategically with personality matching is worth it.

THE ASSURED SALESPERSON

When it comes to the **A** ↔ **E** match, as noted previously, you have energy in common.

The **A** ↔ **P** partnership has two things in common: You're both task- and goal-oriented.

The **A** ↔ **K** match was not made in heaven; you are opposites. What you need to watch out for is the **A**'s natural impatience with a **K**'s slower decision-making style. You may wonder repeatedly, "Why won't he make a decision? What's the problem?" The **K** you are calling may feel rushed if you are not careful to curb your tendency to push. Also, remember that the **K** is very loyal, and it will take you more time to get him or her away from a competitor.

With this match, if you give up too soon, you will *never* get the business. However, the importance of the account should govern how far beyond your frustration level you are willing to go before moving on.

THE KIND SALESPERSON

For the **K** salesperson, the **K** ↔ **E** match has relationships in common; you both like people. That's always a good start.

Ks and **P**s both want facts and don't move impulsively. This will work in your favor.

Ks and **A**s are opposites! The **A** will seem bossy and rushed to you. He or she will be abrasive and demanding in your eyes and will especially resent your desire to chat. Offer the **A** only the immediately relevant information and tie it directly to his or her goal.

Something that might help you deal with the **A** is to stand up when you are talking on the phone with this type of customer. Walking around the room as you talk will force you to display more energy and enable you to set a faster pace. **Assured Customers** need to hear confidence to conduct business.

The Payoff

Once you have mastered the art of recognizing your customers' personality types and matching them to your own, you'll find your telephone sales calls going much more smoothly. You'll be in tune with your customers and your sales strategies will flow naturally from this harmony.

Finally, the P/E/A/K salesperson—those of you who don't score as an exact fit for any of the four types—has an advantage. You will be able to move more easily among your different style customers. Just be careful that as you slip in and out of your different presentation modes, you don't get too cocky.

Being good at establishing a quick rapport with everybody does not necessarily mean you are the most strategic at closing the business. A more conscious awareness of the needs of each of the types will help you take all types to the next level and sell more over the phone.

Now that Alesia has learned some matching techniques, let's see how she's doing:

CUSTOMER (answers in monotone): Hello, this is Jackson.

ALESIA: This is Alesia from XYZ. You had asked me to get back to you today about the failure rate as posted by that third-party group.

CUSTOMER: Oh yes, I was expecting your call and I was waiting for that information before we made our decision. We're not going to do anything without data. I'm glad you sent it.

Showing her versatility, we hear her match her next customer's style:

CUSTOMER *(tersely):* This is Fred.

ALESIA: Hi Fred, Alesia. Just a quick call to check with you on your future needs with the upcoming merger.

CUSTOMER: Well, good for you. You're the first rep who's called here who had any idea what was going on. Call me back on Monday at 4:00 and we'll talk.

ALESIA: Monday at 4:00 confirmed. Goodbye.

CUSTOMER: Talk to you then.

CHAPTER 4

Getting Gatekeepers to Work for You

PHONE SALES CHALLENGE – *Jake, a longtime salesman in commercial banking, complains: "I could close twice as much business if it weren't so hard to get the actual decision maker on the phone!"*

If you define a gatekeeper as the person or system that stands between you and your sale, you will encounter a number of different types as you work through your daily sales calls. These may include actual people (PBX or company operators, administrative assistants, and receivers of forwarded calls), voice mail systems, and automated company menus. Bypassing these different gatekeepers requires slightly different strategies, but each type is a barrier you must move beyond in order to get to the real decision makers.

As an example, let's look at what can happen during interactions that salespeople may have with actual people on the phone:

SALESPERSON: Good morning. I'd like to speak with your director of marketing. Is that person around today?

GATEKEEPER: Who is this? Who are you with? And what is this about?

In this example, the salesperson's lack of knowledge allowed the gatekeeper to seize control and put the salesperson on the defensive. When you are on the defensive, you have no credibility and consequently will not get through to the decision maker.

SALESPERSON: Oh, good morning, what a lovely voice you have. This is Jake Shamrock and I'd like to speak with your director of marketing. Would you be a sweetheart and switch me over?

GATEKEEPER: What? I really cannot put you through unless I know what this is regarding.

Ah yes, here is an example of the old "charmer" technique. It's surprising that this guy didn't call the gatekeeper "honey." Comments that are too familiar or are merely empty compliments have no place in the business world, and often don't work. Remember, the person on the other end of the line can't see your perfect hair or your killer smile.

SALESPERSON: This is Jake Shamrock. Connect me with your director of marketing.

GATEKEEPER: Who are you with? I'm not authorized to patch calls through. Do you have the person's name that you're looking for?

Now we have the worn-out "voice of authority" approach. This guy thought that if he sounded stern and no-nonsense, the gatekeeper would be appropriately intimidated and put him through. Wrong! And then, there's always voice mail:

VOICE MAIL: You've reached Ray Davenport's desk. Leave a message.

SALESPERSON: Well, hey Ray, I can't believe I still haven't caught up with you. We've got a great deal on some new corporate CD rates. Call me back. (pause) Oh, this is Jake with NBS Banking. You know the number!

In each of these situations, a more professional approach would have made a dramatic difference in the response the caller received and would most likely have resulted in a connection. Granted, not all first calls will result in a direct transfer to the appropriate decision maker, but the caller stands a much better chance using the right tactic.

To be effective in selling over the phone, you need to acquire the tools necessary to help you engage gatekeepers as partners. For example, to best connect with your gatekeepers, focus on the strategies introduced in chapter 3 outlining how to adjust your approach to different personalities. The ideas work as well when managing your gatekeeper relationships as with your customers.

Engage the Person Answering the Phone

Whenever you reach an individual who is not the intended customer, request in a polite, businesslike manner to be put through to that person. There are different tactics governing your wording and the amount of disclosure that you might offer regarding your reason for calling. The one you ultimately choose will depend on who you are speaking with.

RECEPTIONIST OR CENTRAL OPERATOR

By definition, the receptionist or central operator handles all inbound calls to the company, answering the phone and then transferring each call to the proper person. Depending on the size of the organization or level of responsibility, this person may have a tremendous amount of information or be able to do little more than transfer the caller to the appropriate extension. There are a number of different strategies you might use when dealing with a central operator or receptionist.

Strategy #1: Provide minimal disclosure. In dealing with a small company, offering minimal disclosure is the best technique. When you use a relaxed, casual tone to sound comfortable and expected, the receptionist will often read into your tone and inflection that you are a close personal friend of the person you are asking to speak with:

RECEPTIONIST: ACE Construction, this is Jessica. How may I help you?

SALESPERSON: Jessica! This is Jake Shamrock. Is Rasida around this afternoon?

Strategy #2: Provide partial disclosure. If you are calling a larger company, your best bet may be to offer some information but not a lot of it. The strategy in offering partial disclosure is to prevent whoever is on the phone from refusing to put you through to the individual you are trying to reach. You might want to give your name and company, or perhaps just your name and purpose only. The receptionist or central operator is not a decision maker and likely will not understand the value of what you have to offer:

RECEPTIONIST: Good afternoon, Bi-Marginal Assemblies, how can I help you?

SALESPERSON: Good afternoon. This is Jake Shamrock with NBS, could you connect me with Rasida Sandera in finance, please?

Partial disclosure is most effective if you have a name and department (back to the need for proper customer research).

If you have to give your name and purpose, then you'll want to prepare the description of what you offer in advance:

CENTRAL OPERATOR: Good afternoon, Bi-Marginal Assemblies, how may I direct your call?

SALESPERSON: Good afternoon and thank you. This is Jake Shamrock and I need you to direct me to finance, please.

CENTRAL OPERATOR: And what is this in regards to, Mr. Shamrock?

SALESPERSON: This is about our banking relationship with your firm. Will you connect me, please?

It's important to sound like a professional on a professional mission in all instances. Do not offer your company name if it sounds too sales-y, but be sure to be forthcoming with your own name. Most of the time, receptionists don't ask for company names if you make it sound like the decision maker is a personal friend. If you are asked, simply offer your company name confidently, as if the intended customer would want to hear from your company. You may even disclose what business you are in, if the company name isn't obvious. This approach disarms a nosy receptionist, or one well-trained in restricting noncritical calls.

But always remember to use a friendly voice. Keep in mind that you are talking to someone who is treated like a private branch exchange (PBX) all day. A friendly voice will be welcome as long as you don't overdo it. Remember, too, to give *your* name first. Manipulative salespeople typically don't offer their name, and since receptionists and operators are trained to ask questions in order to screen callers, by exchanging your name for theirs you disarm them by not presenting an invasive front.

Finally, keep in mind that whoever is asking the questions is in control of the call. If the receptionist has to ask questions such as your name, your company, or what the call is in regard to, then that person becomes the controller of the call. We never want to have a barrier between us and the real decision makers. We want to be in control of the call.

> *Strategy #3: Make a scouting, or "recon" call.* This sort of call can be very useful, especially for your first contact with a company. The purpose here is only to get a name—a direct contact—and the company operator can give you valuable information. Don't ask to be put through, although if the operator offers, you can consider it a bonus:
>
> **SALESPERSON:** Hello, this is Jake Shamrock with NBS Banking and I'd like to find out who your director of marketing is.

Strategy #4: Make a follow-up call. Follow-up calls increase the likelihood that you will be put through to the party you are trying to reach. In this case you are using partial disclosure because you have established a relationship with the decision maker, and you assume the receptionist is familiar with that. Remember, only use this wording if it is true. A receptionist who puts through a call under false pretenses gets in trouble, and you have forever closed that gate (Believe me, she'll remember your voice, company name, and maybe even have noted your number from the caller ID.):

SALESPERSON: Jessica! Hi. This is Jake Shamrock. Rasida Sandera wanted me to give her a callback today. Is she in?

Or, you might choose to say:

SALESPERSON: This is Jake Shamrock. I'm returning Rasida's call. What's the best time to catch her in?

Sometimes the receptionist or central operator will put you through, or give you information on when to call back. This individual is an initial contact and has less of a stake in screening calls than other types of gatekeepers.

TALK TIP

Take some time to look over your contact list to be sure you are keeping track of gatekeepers as well. When you review your call day activity, record the reactions you received:

_____ Attitude good
_____ Connected me to decision maker
_____ Responsive to questions
_____ Relationship established/improved

When you take a tactical approach to gatekeepers, you can engage an ally.

ADMINISTRATIVE (OR EXECUTIVE) ASSISTANT

Personal assistants have responsibility for a person or group of people. The assistant's job is to take care of the people to whom he or she reports. If a visiting vice president is on a low-carbohydrate diet, the administrative assistant will ensure that low-carb snacks are on the conference room table for a meeting. This is someone who knows what the bosses are thinking almost before they think of it. He or she can also be your most valuable partner.

Some customers are very dependent on their assistants for not only organizational matters, but also decision making. In some cases, an admin can make decisions on behalf of the boss or help to push decisions through. In our competitive selling environments, where customers are busier than ever, never underestimate the power of an administrative assistant's influence.

Strategy: Treat the assistant as a key decision maker. Assume the assistant will play a central role in getting you to the person who signs the checks. Keep in mind, however, that assistants are well-trained screeners and have heard every trick in the book, so forget about your bag of tricks and employ your professional strategies. Be respectful and engage this person as your internal sales partner, the one who can make or break you. Ask the assistant the same questions you would ask the final decision maker. When you do this, you elevate yourself in that person's eyes by asking meaningful questions and by directing those important questions to him or her. By doing this you are also differentiating yourself from your competition by affirming the assistant's power; and you are doing it over the phone!

It's helpful to find out how the assistant fits into the decision-making picture. How will your product or service affect this person or his or her boss's goals? You may learn, for instance, that this assistant has had to field shipping complaints, which have become a personal irritant. He or she has to either handle or forward these calls and sees this as a time-consuming nuisance. Now that you know what motivates the assistant, you can connect with this person. Connection could become sympathy for the situation or confirmation of the relationship between the decision maker's need and the assistant's discomfort. Get the buy-in from this individual, and he or she will likely help you set up a phone meeting with the decision maker.

Also, use *full disclosure* when an executive assistant who has decision-making authority answers the phone. Identify yourself and explain who you are with and what you are calling about. This is especially important when the assistant is working for a major decision maker.

A Greener Way to Do Business

Gatekeeper relationships can be made just as effectively using the phone as in person. California has committed to reducing gas emissions by 25 percent by the year 2020 and by 80 percent by 2050. Your switch to phone contacts for gatekeepers can contribute to your personal environmental strategy. Green is an active operating style, a set of choices you make. Even the smallest one makes a difference.   *Source: carbonpartner.com*

DESIGNATED ADVISER/RESEARCHER

Another gatekeeper you may meet on the way to a sale could be the key adviser to a decision maker. Although this person doesn't make the actual decision, he or she is very involved in the sales process. Think of this individual as an information-gatherer for the company.

Years ago, the decision maker would call with inquiries when there was a need. Now, however, managers have much more responsibility in terms of numbers of people they manage, and as a result they will delegate the initial search process to an adviser/intermediary. Often these information-gatherers are **P**s—detail-oriented, thorough, and virtually unaffected by emotional decisions.

This type of selling scenario takes longer because you need to sell this individual, who also acts as a screener for the person he or she reports to. Decision makers will not talk with you unless their screener is convinced it's worthwhile and has recommended your product or service. In this situation you must, in effect, persuade an internal agent to sell *for* you.

> *Strategy: Treat this individual as if he or she were the direct conduit to the sale.* Never underestimate the intelligence and potential influence of advisers/researchers. They will be both highly skilled and professional, which is why they are chosen as screeners. Respected as subject matter experts, they are generally the ones on whom the decision maker relies for information and recommendations.

At times you may find that an intern has this level of expertise and respect in a company. For example, the intern emails you for information on your product. Eventually, you get the intern on the phone. Because an intern is not as invested in keeping people out and is often flattered to have a phone call, you may obtain a great deal of recon-rich information from him or her.

Whatever capacity the adviser/researcher is in officially, he or she is the one who can make or break you. Think of it this way. They are like the first door into the lobby. You don't get to the sixth floor unless the lobby door is unlocked.

ROLLOVER OR CALL FORWARD—COLLEAGUE OR EMPLOYEE

Typically, in a smaller office there might be a vice president and a few managers. This could be a regional office of a larger organization. So, when a decision maker is out, he or she may just set the call forwarding to whoever is going to be in the office at that time. As the one who is just answering the phone when your customer is out, this person doesn't feel any great responsibility for relaying the urgency of a message. For instance, someone in accounting might receive a rolled-over call for human resources.

> *Strategy: Recognize that your forwarded call is an intrusion*

but it may be your only link to your customer. Typically, this individual may answer with just the company name, or their name. This means you will be unaware of whether you're speaking to a marketing assistant, human resources manager, vice president, or operations director. In this case, glean what personality information you can from the voice, adjust your minimal disclosure energy level and tone accordingly, and proceed. In short, every answered phone is an opportunity to get to your decision maker if handled skillfully.

It's best to provide *minimal disclosure* by offering only your name and the name of the person you are calling. Once again, use your warm, friendly voice and make it sound as though you are calling your very best friend in the world. The likelihood of getting through will be significantly increased.

GATEKEEPER PARTNERSHIPS

As you can see, in several of the previous possible call scenarios, you are going to be challenged to have a conversation with an intermediary. Intermediaries can, intentionally or unintentionally, make your job a lot tougher. You need to engage them in partnerships with you—either temporary or long term, depending on the situation. *And* you generally have only a few seconds to process that situation and strategize the best course of action.

In the example that follows, you'll see how the salesperson maintains a listening and professional strategy and is therefore able to uncover a business need.

> **SALESPERSON:** Angela, I'm sure you're very busy. (Pause here just a second or two to see if Angela wants to tell you how busy she is.)

> **GATEKEEPER:** Why, as a matter of fact I am. Tracking my boss's paperwork for travel expenses takes a lot of my time over and above my regular work.

> **SALESPERSON:** I can understand. Our company has some really easy-to-use software that even your boss might feel comfortable with. Would that help you at all?

You see, just the fact that you acknowledged the duress many receptionists and assistants are under will differentiate you from other callers, who may treat them like voice mail. It only takes a few seconds to be supportive, and support, unlike flattery, is always welcome. As a result, in that call or other calls that will follow you can likely expect a cooperative reception.

For example, let's say you are returning a call from a customer and reach a receptionist:

> **SALESPERSON:** Keisha! Michael called me earlier. I'm trying to reach him, and I hope you can help me out. He said to call him at ten, but I haven't been able to get in touch with him. Do you mind paging him, or should I call back this afternoon?

In this scenario, the gatekeeper might, as a consequence of your approach, feel sorry for you, appreciate your honesty, and find the contact for you or give you a better number—cell or other location. As a sales professional, you can differentiate yourself from others who call and aren't professional.

A note here about formality. The more formal approach can be more effective, meaning that you should call a person by Mr. or Ms. and use their surname. With receptionists and administrative assistants, however, we often have only their first name. They may answer the phone with, "Alexander Courtney's office, this is Pat." Or even say, "This is Kevin." Thus, calling Pat or Kevin by a first name would not likely be perceived as being too familiar or unprofessional. If you have a last name, such as Ms. Kendall, then address the admin in that way. Also, remember, when someone answers with their name, include that information in your CRM or notes for future reference. Incidentally, if the administrative professional fails to answer with his/her name, make sure you ask at the end of the conversation by using this question: "Thanks for your help, and tell me your name again, please?" That way, you get the name from the person, but it doesn't sound intrusive, and next time you can say, "Hello Kevin, I'm trying to reach Michael . . ."

As in so many of our examples, professional tone is important.

Treating a decision maker's assistant with respect instead of contrived familiarity will help you to stand out among others who call with the "cheesy" approach.

Use Voice Mail to Gain Useful Information for Strategic Calling

Think of voice mail as the automation that most individuals and companies use to announce who they are as well as to accept messages. Conversely, it may be the customer's first introduction to you. Let's look at how personality assessment plays into your voice mail strategy—not only in the way you leave strategic voice mails for your customers, but also in the hints customers' voice mails give you.

PERSONALITY AND VOICE INFLECTION

You can often get all the information you need to best match the new customer's personality style from his or her voice.

> *Strategy: Listen to your customer's voice mail announcement.* There is a lot you can learn about your customer by listening to the voice mail recording. If you know you need to make an important call on Tuesday to Jose Juarez, a very solid lead, call his voice mail late at night, when you know he isn't there, and listen to his message, so you can prepare for the call the next day. Using this method, you will be able to listen and learn his personality style from the voice mail clues. It will be as if you already know him through his voice, and it will allow you to better plan for your call the next day.

As you listen, pay attention. Does he sound assertive and brusque, or more passive? An assertive tone sounds forceful, confident, perhaps hurried, direct, clear, and even abrupt. A passive tone might sound more hesitant, careful, perhaps detail-oriented, includes more filler words ("uhm," "er," etc.), and typically contains pauses. This assertive versus passive determination is the first-level screen for you to identify the customer's real personality type—in advance of having a conversation.

If the voice sounds assertive, the customer will be an **Assured** or an **Energized;** if passive, the customer is either a **Kind** or a **Precise.**

The next clue you need to listen for is whether this person sounds abrupt, friendly, or upbeat:

- The **P** sounds more monotone, remote, and possibly disinterested. ("You've reached Jose Juarez; leave a message or email me at juarez@abcnet.com.")
- The **E** sounds more upbeat and animated, comparatively. ("This is Jose. Since I missed your call, leave me a message and I'll call you back. Thanks a lot.")
- The **A** sounds terse. ("This is Jose, leave me a message.") Notice how short the message is. As do not like to waste time; they thrive on accomplishing tasks quickly. You might note that many As also record their phone messages from their mobile phones (often on their way to the airport and going through a tunnel!).

If the customer sounds passive, he or she is a **P** or **K.**

- The **K** sounds warm, calm, happy, and fairly detailed ("Hello, you've reached the voice mail of Jose Juarez. Sorry I missed you. You may leave me a message and I'll call you back just as soon as I return to my desk later this afternoon. Have a nice day.")

The challenge for you as a sales professional is that in a real-time call, you have only two or three seconds to determine the personality type if you haven't already gleaned that from a prior contact or the customer's voice mail. For this reason, prime yourself before each call to be ready to analyze and respond to a voice interaction. Be patient with yourself as you become accustomed to this process. You will learn to respond more quickly just by practicing. It helps, though, if you are free of distractions each time and are listening at a deep level so you can concentrate.

LEAVING A MESSAGE

So many times we have to settle for leaving a voice mail rather than having an actual conversation with our customer. You can, however, make this type of contact work for you with these useful strategies.

> *Strategy: Leave a voice mail message consistent with the customer's personality.* You have already heard your customer's voice mail message, and decided on a personality type. Now make the match. Your tone, inflection, speed, energy level, amount of detail, rhythm, and approach should be consistent with the customer's natural style. Doing this, you are more likely to elicit a returned call.

The **P** sounds monotone, unemotional, and low energy. They typically do not like to communicate over the telephone. Email is their preferred contact method. So it stands to reason that they sound as if it is almost painful to use the phone. This impression does not necessarily equate to their character or general happiness, but it does typify the way they communicate over the telephone. If you are a high-energy person, you will need to speak more slowly and deliberately for the **P**. Keep your message brief—between seven and twelve seconds—but resist the urge to speak too fast. If that's too much pressure for you to do on the fly, prepare in advance with some sort of outline for a message that fits that person, such as:

> "Hi, this is Renee Walkup from SalesPEAK, and I'm calling to briefly discuss your sales team. Call me at 678-587-9911."

Remember to say your number S-L-O-W-L-Y. You are used to the number, but your recipient is not. No one will play the message several times to try to make out a garbled phone number. Even though that is generic as a message, you will need to change the energy level and tone to match the personality of the person on the other end.

For **E**s, you'll want to match their style with an energetic, lively, compelling message. Use clear enunciation and an upbeat rhythm. These customers enjoy excitement and want to hear enthusiasm in your voice, tone, and inflection. Just remember to slow down when you leave your phone number! Your message may sound like this:

> "Hi Kathy, it's Renee Walkup with SalesPEAK and I wanted to get your opinion on an opportunity. Call me back at 678-587-9911. Thanks, Kathy, and I look forward to hearing back from you."

For **A**s, you'll match them with extreme confidence; be clear and quick. Use strong words, such as "need," "have to," and "call me." Remember, "uhms" and pauses will make you sound less confident and professional. An **A** will pick up on this immediately. Also, avoid leaving a lengthy message. **A**s are the customers who are the least patient and have the shortest attention span, which includes voice mail. Leave a message similar to this:

> "Gary, this is Renee Walkup with SalesPEAK. Call me at 678-587-9911."

The **K** prefers pleasantries and a calm, warm, and friendly-sounding voice. Don't hurry. Take your time with your message; feel free to include as much detail as necessary, and you'll find that you build rapport just in your voice mail. Avoid sounding too hurried, pushy, or "cheesy." These customers need to hear sincerity and caring in your tone. Your message may sound like this:

> "Robin, hi. This is Renee Walkup with SalesPEAK. Hope you're having a good day. Give me a call at 678-587-9911 so we can discuss an idea that may interest you. Thanks, Robin."

When you practice leaving personality-specific voice mails you build your flexible communication skills, which will allow you to engage and secure the attention of more customers than you likely do now. If you can't get them on the phone, you can't sell them!

DIRECT FIRST-PERSON VOICE MAIL

When you are sure that you have your customer's personal voice mail, you can leave a customized message that will support your selling process.

Strategy: The message you leave should last no more than twelve or thirteen seconds. No matter how much you would like to give your entire "pitch," don't! Do, however, be certain that you speak distinctly and leave a very clear message. If calling from a landline, your entire message will likely be clear, as long as you take the time to say your number slowly. If from a cell phone, you might repeat your phone number. Not everyone checks caller ID and you want the customer to make the return call.

Watch out, though, for this scenario: Shoko says: "I've got about a half hour before my next appointment; I'm going to make some cold calls."

This is a good use of Shoko's time, but she took out her Black-Berry when a landline phone was right there on her desk. We forget sometimes that we are infinitely clearer on the landline. For a test, call your own phone and leave yourself a message from your cell and then from your landline.

You might argue, "I like to use my BlackBerry for the call record." But what's more important—the record or clarity? Mobile phone devices provide convenience, but not necessarily strategic effectiveness. Break yourself of the adolescent need to have your mobile phone permanently attached to your hand. Business is about securing sales from customers, not about being able to chat while you're at the drive-up window at the local fast food restaurant. Effectiveness of communication, not necessarily ease of communication, is the goal for the phone salesperson.

VARIATION ON VOICE MAIL: RIGHT CUSTOMER, WRONG VOICE

Even when you've been directed to your customer's desk phone, occasionally you hear someone else's voice and not your customer's.

Strategy: Use the clue to approach this new gatekeeper. When the outgoing message is in the voice of someone of the opposite sex, it's obvious that this isn't your customer. It's possibly an assistant, very likely a gatekeeper. You know immediately to try to get a receptionist or someone else on the phone.

You now have a new hint: an additional gatekeeper is involved; there is a person between you and your customer, not just voice mail. Identify yourself and say, "I noticed that Matt isn't answering his own phone. Can you tell me the best way to reach him?"

Sometimes the person will give you an alternate number—including a mobile phone number!

If a male voice says, "This is John Jones's line; please leave a message at the tone," can you assume it's John's voice? In this situation, too, you might try to reach a receptionist or John's assistant. You'll want to confirm in your call notes whether John has a male assistant.

COMPUTER-GENERATED MAILBOX RECORDING

A computer-generated mailbox recording may be technically required by a phone system, or it's possible that the person is such a high **P** that he or she hates the phone communication. This customer will leave their name only to be substituted into the programmed message. In some cases, the reason for the computer-generated message is that the customer is an **A** who doesn't want to waste time recording a message because he or she is too busy doing much more important things.

> *Strategy: Listen to the energy level in the recorded voice.* There is some differentiation in energy among personality styles even when they are only saying their name. When you leave a message, use an even, generic voice and tone—not too energized or too slow—but use strong words to create a sense of urgency without sounding like it's an emergency.

COMPANY AUTOMATED MENU (*NO* INFORMATION)

Many companies are going the automated menu route to save money on receptionists or PBX operators. Perhaps you simply hear a robotic extension number or a computer-generated voice. Here are two ways you might deal with an automated menu:

1. One approach is to listen for the options to reach a receptionist, and take the time to follow the menu to get to the person's extension. If the specific extension for your customer is not on a list, opt for another person to help you secure the exact extension or number. Even if you get the wrong person, he or she might be inclined to give you the number—rather than transfer you to a receptionist, who has been trained to keep people (like us) out.

2. Another approach is to punch any number until a human answers, and then ask for the person you are targeting by title or name. Call the president's office if you have to, and when an administrative assistant answers the phone, ask for help or to be transferred. You can also contact the sales department and speak with a salesperson, since salespeople are open and likely to be helpful. They might even give you some information that would be useful for your sale.

The Payoff

Getting to customers is one of the biggest challenges of phone selling. Learning to manage gatekeepers as well as other obstacles such as alternate contact media will help you fast track to your contacts. Once you get to your customers, you have the opportunity to do what you do best—*sell to anyone over the phone.*

Let's see what Jake has learned.

JAKE: Hi, this is Jake Shamrock and I'm calling from NBS Banking. I'd like to get the name of the director of marketing. Can I get that from you?

OPERATOR: Oh, that's Julia Walthers. Would you like me to see if she's in?

JAKE: Good morning, this is Jake Shamrock from NBS Banking. How do you spell your marketing director's name? I'm trying to send an email and it keeps coming back.

RECEPTIONIST: It's Julia Walthers. Most people leave out the aitch.

JAKE: Hello, this is Jake Shamrock from NBS Banking. I'm calling because we have a new online payment process that might be able to help your marketing department. What's the best way to get in touch with your marketing director?

RECEPTIONIST: I don't know if they're interested or not, but you would need to speak with Julie Walthers on that and I'll switch you to her voice mail. (In some cases they may respond with an email address: J.Walthers@eaglesearth.com)

JAKE: Can you give me that extension number in case I get lost in the transfer?

RECEPTIONIST: Certainly. It's 4751.

JAKE: Thanks.

CHAPTER 5

Asking High-Value Questions

PHONE SALES CHALLENGE – *Maria, from IT staffing services, has a problem: "I would really like to get more information from customers, but over the phone they just seem to be distracted or clam up after I ask a question, like they aren't even there. Sometimes all I get is monosyllabic grunts that don't help me at all."*

Maria isn't the only salesperson making mistakes that hinder her effectiveness. Look at what these other callers are saying:

SALESPERSON: Who makes the decision on your company's IT staffing?

CUSTOMER: Not me; you'll have to talk to somebody else.

The problem with this question is that if the customer says that he or she is the decision maker, then that's an open invitation for what is perceived as a long "spiel" from an interrupting caller. The hand-off response gives you no information at all—if the person on the other end of the phone truly isn't the decision maker, you need to know who is. This caller obviously hadn't established a connection with the customer and had crossed a line, with the result that the customer felt invaded.

SALESPERSON: Why can't your company change vendors since your fiscal year is just about up?

CUSTOMER: That's our policy. Sorry I can't help you. Goodbye.

Again, the caller asked an invasive question that actually sounds accusatory and argumentative. "Why" questions are generally dead ends.

SALESPERSON: Do you know what companies are on your IT staffing approval list?

CUSTOMER: Why would I have that information? Call purchasing.

Clearly this caller hadn't done the proper background work and had contacted the wrong person. Although information was gained on this call, the salesperson lost this contact's goodwill for the future.

SALESPERSON: Can you change suppliers anytime you want to?

CUSTOMER: No, that's a lot of hassle and we just went through it with our current one.

Ouch! Instead of discovering the company's process for purchasing (a valuable piece of sales information), this caller merely jabbed what already appears to be a sore spot. With this, the caller has no place to go with any other questions, so even if the supplier could be changed with an easier process and even if the salesperson's products are indeed better, this call is pretty much over.

The point that you want to get to in your sales calls is a conversational harmony with an eventual joining of purpose, which leads to the sale. For this reason, every question should add value to your information-gathering strategy. High-value questions help you to get to the money more quickly. As a bonus, they are very effective in shortening the customer's time on the phone, so that he or she becomes more likely to take future calls of yours. No chitchat or time-wasting questions from you! Your customers will appreciate your willingness to get to the point—their problem—by a direct route.

Establish or Deepen Your Relationship with the Customer

In a conversational sales approach you, as the sales professional and product expert for your company, begin by gathering information and establishing, or deepening, the relationship with your customer. However, customers don't like the feeling of being interrogated or being "sold." Customers like to *buy*. And that's okay, because you aren't selling in the old, strong-arm way. You're building a relationship based on mutual respect, and conversing with a customer whose business or bottom line will be enhanced by a product or service you are offering. You just need to find out how the process to purchase will work, present the solutions your company offers, and then close. High-value questions are necessary in effective phone selling.

AVOID LEADING WITH PERSONAL QUESTIONS

What has been traditionally taught and what worked in the old days, for example, was asking personal questions to build rapport at the outset of the sales call. Today, this kind of chitchat sounds amateurish; it also jeopardizes the business relationship early on by wasting the customer's valuable time. Today's busy customers rarely spend time with their closest loved ones, so they don't usually welcome making new friends over the phone. Why would you think a person would welcome being interrupted from the demands of a business day for a *non*-business-sounding call?

Customers may resent being pulled into a personal conversation at work and with strangers, but they *will* pay attention to information and questions about their business. You can become an integral part of the success of their business, but they don't necessarily want to be involved with you personally. A solid, reciprocal business connection is all you need, and all that your customers want until you've reached an appropriate point in your relationship.

That is not to say that a business/personal relationship never occurs. Many of us likely have personal friends we met through work.

(In fact, the two authors of this book first met professionally, then developed a personal and business relationship.) But if this sort of relationship does occur, it will grow naturally with people to whom we are attracted; it will not be created by artificial plays at friendship with customers.

Today, a warm opening is followed by a cogent question in a businesslike tone. Avoid: "Hi, how's the wife and kids?"

AVOID OPENING WITH TRANSACTIONAL QUESTIONS

On the other hand, the sales conversation is not merely a transaction either. Transactional selling says, "I've got a product; you've got $5. Let's do business." This is why we avoid questions like, "Are you the decision maker?" or "Do you have a $50,000 budget?" To the customer, these questions sound like this: "Do you have any buying-decision power or are you just the flunky, because I'm after the big dog." Or, "How much money do you have, so I know what I can go after?"

Can you see why these questions generally fail to produce cooperation? As openers, they rarely earn you the chance to complete the call or get a callback. They aren't relationship-building questions. In transactional selling, the situation is clearly about you and what you want. Customers get enough of that treatment from their bosses and from other salespeople. Questions that make it clear that you are interested in what the *customer* might want will take you a long way toward the close.

Every contact with a customer is a relationship. Whether it's a one-call close or long-term business, some form of relationship must exist for you to make a sale. To achieve sustained sales, the relationship must be positive.

Use Questions as Tactics

If you are in sync with your customer, you are questioning and learning, and then becoming part of the input for the purchase decision. This makes you a *partner*. Customers will rely on you for information, and you'll be able to rely on them for sales you can close over the phone. When you understand the way questions can help (as well as how they can hurt) your sales calls, then each time you use one, you can feel more secure in the outcome.

Your goal is to get your customer singing off the same song sheet with you. How do you do that? By using a specific process of qualifying that builds rapport, establishes your credibility, and maximizes your opportunities for closing the sale.

QUESTIONS QUALIFY

Let's take a slightly different look at the qualifying portion of the sales call. If you fail to qualify well, you dramatically reduce your ability to close. You begin the qualifying process by guiding the customer to making his or her own buying decision, because today's customers don't want to be told what to buy. This process involves you leading the customer to make that decision through strategic qualifying questions. Your goal is to gain the customer's attention by asking the right high-value questions.

Your strategic qualifying tactics should do the following:

- Establish your credibility as an expert in the customer's situation.
- Uncover your customer's real needs.
- Deepen your customer relationships.
- Lay out a foundation for how you are going to present your sales solutions.

If you don't qualify well, you won't get the customer's attention. Remember, customers are busy and are not really thinking about buying your product or service when the phone rings. The way you ask questions indicates to customers whether you are interested in their business and whether you are listening—*really* listening.

QUESTIONS ESTABLISH CREDIBILITY

If the customer does not already know you, your strategic questioning will establish credibility if the questions have been well thought out in advance. The presentation that follows qualifying is where you share your idea of a solution, so it's critical that your credibility already be established. Qualifying must be done both early and correctly because your *intelligent* qualifying differentiates you from other salespeople, and that's what we all want—differentiation. If you are unable to differentiate yourself from the others who call on your customer, you won't get the sale. Remember that "intelligent" (as a credibility definer) means "directly relevant to the customer's business."

For example, if you are selling to someone in the newspaper or printing business, you might ask, "Can you tell me how you handle your wasted paper?"

This is an intelligent question because wasted paper is a concern in those industries, and by asking a relevant question you have shown that you know the customer's business. Note that we used the word "tell" at the start of the qualifying, and we used the second person, "you" or "your," twice in one sentence.

QUESTIONS UNCOVER CUSTOMER NEEDS

You uncover needs by asking questions to help lead the customer to making his or her own decision to use your product or service. Think of yourself as a detective. Here are some examples of questions you might ask:

- "Tell me about your existing situation."
- "What is the application (purpose or use)?"
- "Where is the installation?"
- "Tell me, how is this going to be implemented?"
- "Who will be using these products?"
- "What other products are you currently using?"

Sometimes your questioning can help customers uncover needs they didn't know they had. When this happens, you confirm your position as a consultant who can contribute in a meaningful way to the success of your customer's business. Thus, product or service recommendations you make after that point will be well received, and you are on your way to longer-term business. The reason is that the customer is being led down the path of buying your solution—not by you talking about all your great products, but by assisting the customer in making his or her own decision. The added advantage of this strategy is that once customers make their own decisions, they rarely renege on a commitment.

QUESTIONS DEEPEN RELATIONSHIPS

As your questions are well thought out, your customer will most likely be impressed with your ability to pin down the challenges that your product will solve. In addition, customers are used to being "talked at" by your competition regarding how great their products are. You will rise above the fray by deepening your customer relationships and asking more strategic questions. But you need to ask the *right* questions—not the *wrong* ones!

A Greener Way to Do Business

The benefits to your company of reducing greenhouse emissions by using the telephone to qualify in lieu of traveling include:

- Lower energy costs.
- Lower material consumption.
- Lower travel expenses.
- Lower travel-related frustration for employees.
- Higher "green" profile for your company or brand.
- Secure position vis-à-vis regulation compliance.

Source: carbon-partner.com

Avoid Asking the Wrong Questions

If you ask the wrong question or ask a too-personal question too soon, customers will cut you off, and you'll never get back in again. Think of it like this: If you were to purchase a new refrigerator and the salesperson asked you how much money you had as an opening question, wouldn't you feel a bit put off?

In the qualifying stage, note that asking, "How are you?" is not a good opening question because we truly don't care, and the customer knows we don't care. Plus, the customer's immediate thought is "Oh, no! Another inexperienced salesperson!" By taking this approach, you can open up yourself for failure from the beginning.

If, for instance, the customer answers your "How are you?" question with "Terrible!" or ignores the question altogether, he or she has taken control of the call and your game has been thrown off. Such a routine and potentially damaging question can also cause you to be seen as flaky when you want to be perceived as knowledgeable and in control. Break this habit if you have it!

You want to ensure that each of your qualifying questions is well thought out to maximize interaction with and information from your customer. When questions are too personal too quickly, customers freeze. You hear it in their hesitation to respond. If your customers freeze on a question, consider your timing (read on for more on this).

There are other questions you should not ask as well, even though you may have heard them from other sales sources. After each of the "freeze" questions that follow, note the better alternatives to use in sales calls.

FREEZE QUESTION #1: "WHAT DO YOU KNOW ABOUT US?"

This is a "me, me, me" question and assumes that knowledge of your company will make the sale. Probably not. In addition, you have put your customer on the spot. Making your customer feel uncomfortable isn't a good way to build a relationship leading to sales. Also, it sounds like a test question. No one likes those. Alternative qualifying questions will build better rapport and get a more honest answer:

- "Tell me about the products you are currently using."
- "What type of buying patterns do you typically have each month?"
- "Can you tell me about your situation?"

FREEZE QUESTION #2: "WHAT WILL IT TAKE TO GET YOUR BUSINESS?"

Asked as an early question, before needs or credibility or relationship are established, this is a sure dead end. The answer you will invariably force from the customer is, "Uh, nothing." The implied message in your question is that you will do *anything* to get their business. Think through the logic here: Are you willing to drive to Montana and personally deliver the goods, or provide free service for a year, or lower your price to less than cost? If you aren't willing to make these types of commitments, don't ask your customer this question. Plus, it sounds cheesy because the customer knows it's insincere. At any point, even later in the call, it can create discomfort, so why use it? Alternatives might include:

- "What is your time frame for making a decision on this project?"
- "What else might you need to take this recommendation to your colleagues?"
- "How can I make your decision-making process easier?"

FREEZE QUESTION #3: "HOW MUCH MONEY DO YOU WANT TO SPEND?"

For customers, the ideal for this is "nothing." Perhaps this question is intended to establish budget, but instead it just reminds the customer that he or she is probably spending more than desired—even if it's on something that is needed. Such a question might also be taken as an insult, leading the customer to respond with, "None of your business." In any event, any customer answer would be misleading, because there is no buying relationship yet. And for that matter, why would a customer tip his or her hand that early? Alternatives could include:

- "Tell me about your budget range."
- "What are your price expectations for this installation?"
- "When you purchased last time, what was the price range?"

FREEZE QUESTION #4: "WHO MAKES THE DECISION?"

There's nothing like insulting the customer with a frontal attack. This question implies that the customer you're speaking with doesn't have the authority or the intelligence to make a decision. So, not only have you insulted your customer but you have set yourself up for failure because the insulted customer's response may or may not be true. The main problem is that you have risked alienating the customer, and the likelihood of making the sale is reduced or eliminated. You also don't know who the decision makers really are. Alternatives are:

- "Tell me about your decision-making process."
- "What method of selecting a vendor do you use?"
- "How are you going to make your decision?"

How do you know what a good question is? If a customer is responding and offering information, then it is a high-quality question. If you feel that the energy on the other end of the phone is going well, then your qualifying questions are most likely on the right track.

Guidelines for High-Value Questions

The basic concept behind high-value questions is: the four **W**s and **H** and **T**.

W questions include who, what, when, where, but *never* why. Why questions put customers on the defensive. Think of it this way: All small children ask, "Why?"—16,000 layers of "why." Also, children are chastised with "Why did you do that?" and "Why can't you get it right?" The word "why" is all too often used in an accusing way. It's an annoying question as well, so drop it from your vocabulary!

Good **W** questions include:

- "*Who* is going to be using the product at your company?"
- "*What* departments are involved during installation?"
- "*When* is the ideal time for implementation?"
- "*Where* are you planning on storing the extra stock?"

H (how) questions are great for understanding a process and application:

- "*How* is the workload distributed?"
- "*How* are the two departments involved in the decision?"
- "*How* are these materials applied?"
- "*How* many do you anticipate needing in the next twelve months?"

The very best, though, are the **T** (tell) questions. Okay, for all you grammarians out there, we know that a sentence that starts with "Tell me" is technically a command or request, not a question. But since questioning is the part of the phone selling process that gathers information from the customer for the purposes of helping us meet needs with our products, we're going to take a little license here and group the "Tell me . . ." phrasing in this question section.

The reason for this is that after twenty years, I realize the tell-me questions are the most effective because they encourage customers to talk. (Remember, when the customer is talking, he or she is selling him- or herself to *you* because you are listening, right? You *are* listening, aren't you?) When asked the right questions, customers enjoy sharing experiences, telling stories, and relating needs. Also, you will find that by asking more **T** questions, you can often learn more about your customer's needs in less time.

When you learn what is on the customer's mind, you are most likely to solve the customer's problem. Of course, you can't use "Tell me . . ." for every sentence, just as you wouldn't use a single one of the **W**s or the **H** before each and every qualifying question (gotta mix 'em up, of course—but you already knew that!). The **T** is golden because once you get in the habit of asking more of these questions, you'll find the necessity of asking too many questions—which may sound like an interrogation—eliminated. We want to ask only high-value questions.

Finally, remember never to interrupt your customer after asking a question, even if the phone silence is uncomfortable. Respect your customer's communication style by being quiet after asking a question and resisting the urge to either answer for the customer or prompt an answer.

> **TALK TIP**
>
> Use the "tongue trick" to stay quiet. Just gently place your tongue behind your front teeth. Let that serve as a reminder to be quiet until the customer is finished speaking.

Your **P** and **K** customers are most likely to hesitate after hearing a question. Remember, these personality types are generally more passive and don't blurt out information quickly. They are used to being interrupted by less professional salespeople. Differentiate yourself by letting these customers process the question and respond— without *you* interrupting them!

Just as an experiment, make a list of as many of your qualifying questions as you can think of that you use regularly. Then go back and change them (if needed) to who, what, when, where, how, or tell (but *not* why).

It is not enough, however, just to get the right questions. The real test of merit for the professional salesperson is to know *when* to ask each question. A money question is necessary at some point for a sale, but asking it at the wrong time kills the relationship. Qualify— but in the *right* order.

Ask Questions at the Right Time: The Trust Scale

The secret to getting a customer responding and eating out of your hand is to begin with easy, broad, nonthreatening questions to put him or her at ease in the call.

Instead of asking, "When did you last finance this equipment?," try, "How are you handling payments now?" Keep it simple; become more specific as you go along to bring in focus. Whether your product is running shoes, insurance, building supplies, or help desk services; whether you are dealing with a new customer or it's the fiftieth call, *the pattern is the same*. Simple, non-invasive qualifying questions always come first, more complex ones come later in the call.

What so many salespeople forget is that the questions most important to them are the most personal to the customer. For this reason, the typical salesperson jumps the gun and sabotages the call. The most personal and most potentially unsettling for the customer are questions about money or time because people's values (in business and in their personal lives) are determined by how they spend their money and time. As a sales professional, whatever product or service you are selling has either a money or time (or both) component to the close.

Think of your qualifying strategy as a trust scale (see Figure 5-1). The more detailed the question, the more it belongs *after* the customer has relaxed during the call. After all, customers don't want to feel like the call is an interrogation, and you don't want to feel like an interrogator!

To avoid this type of adversarial situation, ask your easy, non-threatening questions first. Think of these as level 1–3 questions.

Your mid-level questions—for example, those relating to issues with existing conditions, the competition, and so forth—should be considered level 4–7 questions on the trust scale. These questions require that the customer is more relaxed before he or she will answer honestly.

Your most personal or threatening questions—those requiring trust before your customer will answer candidly—fall on the high end of the trust scale—between levels 8 and 10—and generally involve money. Think of it like this: If you ask me how much money I have to invest, I may tell you, but I won't do it at the beginning of a phone call. I'll need to know that I can trust you before providing that level of information.

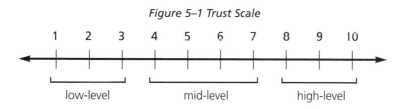

Figure 5–1 Trust Scale

Level 1–3 questions produce little anxiety for the customer.
These are broad and nonthreatening questions, ones that

make the customer feel at ease so he or she will offer more information:

- "Can you tell me about your existing situation?"
- "Tell me how you've handled this challenge in the past."
- "Who will be using the product?"
- "When are you considering implementation?"

Level 4–7 questions usually have to do with competition. These questions provide some frame of reference on decision-making process:

- "What's worked for you using your existing supplier?"
- "If you could change the current process, what would you do differently?"
- "Tell me a bit about your decision-making process."
- "What is your decision date?"
- "How many copies/versions do you expect to use?"
- "What other solutions are you considering?"

Level 8–10 questions are more detailed or specific relating to time and/or money. These questions should never occur in the qualifying or discovery part of your sales conversation:

- "Can you tell me your expectations for your contractual budget range?"
- "You mentioned your insurance will pay part of the cost; what is your deductible?"

The latter is a prying question that will be received well *only* if you are already considered a partner in the relationship. If this is your first question, the customer might perceive that price is conditional on insurance. However, if the customer has already offered some specifics about his or her situation, then it is a natural question.

Let's look now at how the trust scale applies to second and third contacts with the same customer. Every engagement with the customer requires that you start at the low end of the scale, even if you feel that the relationship has progressed. Your call structure should not change. It's just like getting dressed: Regardless of what you are wearing or how you are feeling, the routine remains the same –underwear before pants, pants before belt, etc. Repeatedly practicing this process will take some stress off you as the salesperson because you will have an expectation for every call—and your customers will respond because the process and structure put them at ease with you as well.

Here's a call following up on a proposal that was sent:

Question 1: "Since we last spoke, has anything with your buildings changed?" (Level 2 question)

Question 2: "What are your thoughts about the proposal?" (Level 5 question)

Question 3: "We can arrange for you to take a tour of some of the buildings we maintain close to you so you can see our work. How does that sound? (Level 8 question)

Occasionally you might sense that the customer is not listening or is backing off in some way. This can happen at any time in your dealings with a customer, even a long-standing one. You can't know all the boundaries your customer may have, nor can you anticipate or control everything that happens to your customer. Always be on the alert for tension in your customer's voice or wording.

When you sense this tension it can mean that you have asked a question out of order. At these times, interrupt yourself with, "Oh, just let me back up a moment and ask you something else I think I missed earlier." Be sure your tone is much less excited and your pace somewhat slower. You can salvage the call sometimes with this tactic, but there are some questions that you cannot really come back from. These are sales-stoppers.

SERIOUS SALES-STOPPER QUESTIONS

The following situations and questions are guaranteed to stop any conversation with a customer:

- A Level 8, 9, or 10 question asked too soon: "What's your budget?" Or, "Will you buy today?"
- A self-serving question or a threat: "My quota ends today, will you buy?" This is a self-serving question. An example of a threat would be, "Do you know that if you don't make a decision by tomorrow, you'll have to pay more since the price increase will take effect?"
- Disaffirming questions: "Should I contact your boss?" The implication is that the customer cannot possibly have the authority.
- Clichéd or overly restrictive questions: "Is there any reason you can't buy from me today?" Or, "What will it take to get your business?"
- Stupid questions: "How much money do you have?" Or, "If I can show you how to save 50 percent on your bill, will you make a commitment today?"

Your goal should be to make the customer feel that he or she wants to buy rather than that he or she is being sold to.

> **TALK TIP**
> Monitor your questioning patterns with each call. You may be falling into a lockstep pattern of pushy, invasive questions in an attempt to move the sale along more quickly. Speed is of no value if it just hurls you toward a "no." And for a quick check, go through your own qualifying questions, the ones we asked you to look at, evaluate, and rewrite above. Now eliminate any sales-stoppers from your repertoire!

QUESTIONS FOR PERSONALITY STYLES

Different personality styles require some customization of your questioning strategy to allow you to choose the most effective approach.

The **Precise Customer—P**s respond to questions monosyllabically. They give limited information in a monotone voice without elaboration. Seven questions from you might elicit only twenty-four words in response. Ask process/procedural and fact questions. This person, you can be certain, will know the number of stations that will need the software, the users and their levels of expertise, the purchasing procedures, the time for the decision making, and more, much more.

The **Energized Customer**—Es will be thinking about self and effect on self. These customers want to talk more. "How important to you is ease of use?" "How quickly do you need this to be implemented?" "How do we make this easier for you?" "Tell me your impressions of being first in your city to have this product."

The **Assured Customer**—As will give you the same number of words, but will be more emphatic. They are interested in their goals and like to have their authority recognized:

- "When do you expect to make this decision?" (authority)
- "Can you tell me about what you need this software to do?"
- "What do you need to accomplish with this new system?"
- "When are you planning on making the decision to move forward?" (goals)

The **Kind Customer**—Ks will give you a lot of answers relating to the people around them. You can ask them the following type of questions:

- "Can you tell me about what your team has been looking at so far?"
- "Would you share with me how the people in your organization see these products?"
- "How will upgrading your software affect the workers' time?"
- "What training might your employees need once you implement a new product?"
- "How can we help you with a successful installation at your office?"

Sometimes an **Assured** or an **Energized** will hit you with a question first. You need to take control and return to questioning yourself. For example, the customer may say: "So, what do you have that's new today?" or "Can you just tell me about your specials?" or "What do you need?" (on a return call).

Answer by first putting a smile in your voice so that you sound friendly. This is a very important point because it allows you to control the tone of the message: "I'm happy to tell you what we have. But do you mind if I ask you a couple of quick questions first?" Emphasize the words "couple" and "quick" so they know it's not a lengthy process. Then take control of the call by asking a question such as: "What's changed since our last conversation?"

Although there might be some variation in what each type of customer—or even each individual customer—considers a Level 1 or Level 9 question, you still need to remember that a continuum is necessary, because customers are not prepared to answer a Level 9 question without a warm up.

TALK TIP

Remember that whatever your personality type, your tendency will be to ask questions that reflect your natural style. Instead, be strategic and consciously shift your questioning approach to match your customer's personality. Revise your call questions list to include at least four questions for each personality type at each level. Pay specific attention to your choices for the personality types that are different from yours. Make sure you have a good variety of "tell" questions included.

The Payoff

Notice how high-value questions accomplish three important goals:

1. They help you gather information about a customer's situation.
2. They establish a more trusting relationship between you and your customer.
3. They also guide the customer's thinking toward the direction of your service.

Keep your questions low-key and noninvasive, and let them set the stage nicely for the next step in the process: your customized presentation.

Remember that attempts to rush the process by attempting Level 9 or 10 questions too early will not get you to the close more quickly. In fact, the opposite is more likely to happen and, worse, you may not be received well on later, follow-up calls. You can increase your close percentage and turn more calls into sales by respecting the customer's need for process.

Now, let's listen in on Maria's calls to see where she has improved in securing useful information from her customers.

MARIA: Can you tell me about your company's decision-making process when it comes to IT staffing needs?

CUSTOMER: Well, because we operate on yearly budgets we have to submit our project needs and involve human resources. Then we get approval and can start looking for people.

MARIA: When you've established your needs what's the timetable for changing vendors?

CUSTOMER: We work on fiscal year here, regardless of when we really need people.

MARIA: That must be difficult considering some projects. Can you tell me how the IT staffing approval list is working for you?

CUSTOMER: It's creating a problem. What can you do for us?

It looks like Maria has opened a door to dollars by asking the right questions in the right order.

CHAPTER 6

Listening and Presenting

PHONE SALES CHALLENGE – *Matt, a commercial carpet salesman, had this complaint: "Sometimes I tell customers all the great stuff about our line, and they don't say anything. Others talk and talk and I'm bored out of my mind."*

Good salespeople—no, the *best* salespeople—are able to pick up on layers of customer needs, customer personality types, possible objections, and the timing of a close, all on the phone, simply by listening intently. Admittedly, this is a two-part process: focusing sharply enough to catch all the subtle as well as the direct messages the customer sends, and then processing those messages into the best presentation strategy to close the sale.

So, we listen in order to present well, not the other way around. The "features-dump" style of presentation—where the salesperson, speaking quickly, rattles off a list of specifications or perceived benefits of the company's products—is outdated. Customers today are so over this anonymous, unwelcome barrage of verbiage that they will just hang up. But a presentation in which every feature highlights a benefit will go a long way toward getting the decision maker to buy.

In books written to help gals attract a guy, a common thread of advice is (to paraphrase): "Ask questions, pay very close attention to what the guy says, and then during the conversation work his own words back into what you say. When you do this, he will think you are more intelligent." Whether this works in dating or not, it will certainly work with the decision maker on your phone sales call. Customers won't listen to your presentation until you have proven that you're listening to them; a presentation based on hints you have picked up through focused listening will make you sound like a genius!

The first step is *strategic listening* at a deeper level. Look at what happens when you fail to listen:

CUSTOMER: Just give me the bottom line.

SALESPERSON: Well, it has five-gig memory and an adjustable . . .

CUSTOMER (interrupting): Look, are you going to cut to the chase and give me a price or not? I don't have time for this.

The salesperson missed two listening cues from this customer. The first was that she was dealing with an **Assured** personality type. The second was that she continued to rattle off specifications instead of stopping to ask a question or respond with the price. Either way, she lost the attention of the buyer and most likely lost the opportunity to regain it. In the next scenario, the salesperson just creates an objection by not listening to the reluctance in the customer's response:

CUSTOMER: We all participate in the decision.

SALESPERSON: I'd like to come and meet with you personally so we can present how our new service will help you

CUSTOMER: Uh, well, we're really not at that point. You'll have to talk to someone else.

Unwillingness to take on individual responsibility for a sales decision is a classic **Kind** personality behavior. Instead of engaging the customer and asking questions about the decision process and other team members, this sales representative caused the customer to shut down. Not only will there be no sale on this call, but a valuable opportunity to gain critical information has been lost. In the scenario that follows, the salesperson actually irritates the customer.

CUSTOMER: The plan is for us to maintain our relationship with Good Service Company for at least the rest of the contract period, so we are not considering a change at this time.

SALESPERSON: We can cut the price and make it more attractive for you.

CUSTOMER (speaking more loudly): Didn't you hear me? We have a contract. Not interested.

Oh no. The old bulldozer routine that assumes decisions are always about price certainly wasn't effective. If a customer explains that he has a contract for the rest of the year, that's a valuable piece of information. It offers the sales representative an opening to inquire about the contract process and find out what is working and not working about the competitor's product or service. Pay attention!

As a salesperson, you are under pressure to make decisions very quickly about whether to pursue a call or cut your losses and contact a better prospect. This pressure can potentially result in the loss of a sale. Listening strategically over the phone is as essential as being able to talk.

As you are listening, you should be asking yourself some of the following questions:

- Is this customer receptive?
- Is this customer too busy to talk?
- Does this customer sound stressed?
- Is this customer multitasking during your call?
- What is the personality type of the customer?

You need to immediately pick up on your customer's energy. Customers provide you with vocal clues from the first few seconds of your call. These auditory messages are either invitations to move forward or obstacles that require you to slow down.

Listen from "Hello"

When you listen to what your customers are saying once you've got them on the phone, you can quickly read by their language whether they are receptive or whether you should move on. Let's dissect the approaches you would use.

THE EXISTING CUSTOMER

In connecting with existing customers, you are already familiar with how they typically sound and can more readily detect whether their natural personality style is reflected in their voice. Warning signs might include a normally relaxed talker speaking more hurriedly, or an individual who tends to be arrogant and combative suddenly being nonresponsive or subdued. When you detect this change in their normal speaking pattern, you want to engage with a question:

> "Everett, it sounds like you've got a pretty full plate today. Can we schedule this call for a better time?"

> or

> "You sound like you're in a hurry today. When would be a better time to catch you?"

Since you know Everett and are picking up on his inflection clues, this is an opportunity for you to professionally step back and book an appointment for a time when he will be more receptive to listening to you. Don't be the boilerplate salesperson; be the one who engages each customer as a real person. Customers often think we're all alike as salespeople; show them you're not and get the business where others fail.

Remember, though, that this approach is effective only with an existing customer who is familiar with you as well as with your company's offerings and thus may be more willing to work with you. You cannot afford to step away from a new customer without gathering some information from him or her.

THE NEW CUSTOMER

Listen for suggestions of stress in your customer's voice. When people are under stress, their vocal chords tighten, creating a strained quality to their speaking voice. This suggests it may not be the best time to try to engage them in a conversation. In this instance, avoid lagging; simply say, "I have just two quick questions"—and be sure to make them quick, so that you can secure the information you need to for a later appointment.

Suggestions of stress in a new customer's voice can also mean she is distracted. You may hear a lower volume in her voice, or pauses, or whispering or keyboarding in the background. Or there may be a time lag in the response or a clear disconnect with what you are saying. When you find yourself in this situation, use the person's name, ask one or two questions to reengage her, and understand that this is not an opportune time for a features/benefits presentation because she isn't listening in the way you need her to be.

In general, if you detect stress in a customer's voice, you know it's a bad time. Don't try to sell to someone who is under pressure. A nonfocused salesperson who doesn't pay attention to customers' clues and continues to push is less likely to ever connect again because he or she will be remembered as the one who *didn't listen.*

Even on a customer-requested follow-up call, which should be an easy path to a close, you want to be alert. A lack of enthusiasm in the customer's tone can mean any number of things. You'll want to uncover whether this lackluster manner is due to changed conditions concerning the sale or simply a change in mood that has nothing to do with you or your product. If conditions have changed at the customer's end, your job is to regroup quickly and strategize for a new goal. For example, you may decide to set an appointment for a later time when the customer might be more receptive and less distracted.

In addition, keep in mind that the customer's job is to get you off the phone as quickly as possible without your making a sale. That's part of the game of phone selling. Nowhere in the customer's job description is the phrase, "entertain calls from salespeople." Unfortunately, customers have become so accustomed to salespeople who unprofessionally waste their time by telling, telling, and more telling, that they think we *all* talk too much.

Regardless of what businesses those other salespeople represent, they are competing for your customer's time. And that's your *real* competition: time. Your attention to the customer, demonstrated by your listening, can be a differentiator. Are your competitors listening at the same level that you are? Believe me, your customer knows—and purchases accordingly.

Listen for the Customer's Personality Style

When calling a new prospect with whom you don't have an established relationship, listen for the customer's personality style. This is called *strategic listening*, in which you pass from casual listening to a deeper level of attention. You have only a few seconds of effective conversation time to react and choose a strategy suitable to a personality type. The information you gain from this type of listening will determine what you choose to say or do next. You can blow the deal if you try to close when the customer has indicated that an appointment for a later conversation is better. Let's look at the **Precise Customer** first.

THE PRECISE CUSTOMER

Precise Customers tend to sound monotone and speak more slowly, pause often, and hide their emotions. So, you must avoid interrupting even if their answers are maddeningly slow. You need to pause more frequently to allow them to give you something to work with. Listen to the **Ps**' carefully chosen words. Concentrate on the detail clues they are providing you in the call.

You will hear **Ps** use phrases and sentences such as:

- "We'll need test data, proof of your results."
- "We have a lot of expertise in-house, so I'll have to see how you can add to that."

- "I'm not going to paint you a pretty picture."

You'll also hear a lot of words like "documentation," "analysis," "test data," "negotiate," "details," "benchmark," and "proven."

Precise Customers may very well tell you everything you need to do to get the sale. Their message, though, is that the process and needs are all very complex and the information they are giving you should deter you from pursuing the sale. What they don't realize (and you should!) is that they have provided you with a checklist of everything you'll need to prepare to get their business. Listen to the **P** customer carefully and take notes!

THE ENERGIZED CUSTOMER

Energized Customers' messages may throw you off because they are usually open and friendly. Be especially tuned in to the message behind the chatter when an **E** is on the line.

The **Energized Customer** sounds more emotional and hurried whether the situation warrants that response or not. They interrupt and are generally talkative and opinionated. You must listen as energetically as they talk, asking lots of "can you tell me" questions. Allow them to talk and they will volunteer most of what you want to know. Listen carefully for their inflection, because these customers emphasize their real needs.

Phrases and sentences that you'll hear **E** customers say include:

- "We need that information right now!"
- "Lots going on here"
- "Cool new stuff"
- "Good news!"

You'll also hear a lot of words like "excited," "everyone," "relationship," "exceptional," "unbelievable"—and maybe even "awesome," depending on age.

Energized Customers are that way all the time. Don't be fooled by what sounds like enthusiasm for *your* company's product or service. Listen, instead, for any inside information they might let slip.

Since they're talkers, they're not always careful about monitoring what they say.

THE ASSURED CUSTOMER

The **Assured Customer** sounds direct, impatient, and hurried. These customers know what they want and will tell you, usually in an abrupt manner. You'll want to listen to their real needs, and focus your brief presentation on their specific goals. Be prepared to listen, process, and respond quickly, or you will find yourself at the other end of a dial tone.

Phrases and sentences you will hear the **Assured Customer** say in your calls include:

- "What's this opportunity going to cost me?"
- "I've got a great deal from supplier X."
- "Give me the short version."
- "Our strategic initiative is . . ."

They will also pepper their conversations with concepts like "bottom line," "end game," "ROI," "profitability," and "strategic."

When the **A** challenges you with a suggestion that someone has offered a better deal, remember what you're hearing: it's a challenge, not an objection. Listen for the pause that might mean you've said something that has struck home.

Keep in mind, too, that unlike the **E**, the **Assured Customer** *never* slips. Whatever comes out of the **A**'s mouth was intended.

THE KIND CUSTOMER

Kind Customers come off as calm and friendly. When you read the tones in their voice, your inclination might be to sound supportive initially. Listen for hesitation or uncertainty. Since these customers aren't comfortable saying "no" outright, you must listen for more subtle cues. **K**s know that they often get taken advantage of, so they become more cautious buyers. This caution is reflected in their slow and deliberate decision-making style. Words or phrases that **K**s might use are:

- "Others will be involved in the decision."
- "This could take a while."
- "I'm not sure."

Their favorite descriptions of fellow decision makers are "careful," "loyal," and perhaps most of all, "nice person."

The upside is that if you listen carefully, the **Kind Customer**, like the **Precise Customer**, will probably give you all the information you need to pursue the purchase with the other decision makers. The **P**s, though, are much more structured than the **K**s in their communication patterns.

Focus on the Phone: The Listening Challenge

Paying attention to why we, as salespeople, too often fall short of the most effectual listening can help us to turn this shortcoming into a strength. Listening is both a skill and an asset.

Sadly, all too often, we don't listen well for some of the following reasons:

- We have never formally been taught listening as a skill.
- We have short attention spans.
- We multitask while on the phone.
- We begin to steamroll in our enthusiasm.
- We regurgitate product information.
- We are so intent on our next question or comment that we disregard the customer's reaction.

Sound familiar? Now think back to school. (Okay, that may not be a happy thought necessarily, but go with it here for just a moment.) You had courses in reading and writing, history and math, but do you remember taking any listening classes? Most people haven't. And by the way, do you remember receiving any financial reward for listening to what your teachers said? Your high school experience, unfortunately, might have caused you to grow up with more listening-avoidance skills than listening enhancements. You may have even developed a distaste for listening purposefully for a long period of time to anyone who isn't really interesting to you. And we all know that not every customer is interesting to us!

Now, fast-forward to the sales challenges you face every day. Today, years removed from the classroom, the greatest tool you have for your success is the ability to listen to your customer. Let's assess the situation this puts you in: You've never had a serious listening course, but the greatest skill you need to be successful in your job is listening!

Focus on the phone by meeting two major challenges head-on:

1. *Obstacles.* These are challenges—such as multitasking distractions, inability to see customer reactions, restlessness, and fatigue—that can inhibit efficient listening and cause you to lose sales.

2. *Attitude.* Most of us are generally more interested in what we have to say than in what others have to say. We wait impatiently for our chance to speak, especially when we have something else to say and are enthusiastic about the topic.

Since both types of challenges can get in the way of your phone sales success, you need to be able to handle them. This can be done easily with a little self-management.

OBSTACLE CHALLENGES

An obstacle is anything that gets in the way of your listening success. Whether you eliminate obstacles or merely find a way around them, one thing is certain: You cannot afford to ignore them.

Multitasking Distractions. Part of what attracts many of us to the sales profession (besides the *money!*) is that it is a fast-paced, varied, and challenging career. For this reason, we often find ourselves multitasking—for example, using our computer to email while on the phone, placing a sandwich order with a colleague, and making coffee at our desk, all at the same time. Sometimes we get a misguided impression that by multitasking, we are getting more done. Let's take a closer look at this belief.

On the phone, multitasking can be the kiss of death, because if our attention is divided, we are not listening to our customers! When we stop listening, we miss important details that might lead to a sale. When we check email, review our stock portfolio, mouth silent conversations with colleagues, and engage in other activities, our heads are down, and our tone and inflection are impaired. Even rocking in your seat will make you sound different to a customer and affect your ability to listen to the subtleties in the conversation. In addition, these subtle changes in your tone and inflection are heard by the customer on the other end, thereby impeding your ability to gain a rapid rapport.

Solution: Organize and prepare for sales calls. Don't pick up the phone until you have done the following:

- Cleared your desk.
- Turned your chair away from all distractions.
- Closed your door, or put out a "Making Calls—Please Do Not Disturb" sign.
- Turned off audible distractions such as music, the alert tone on email, and your call waiting.
- Prepared yourself to make and/or take calls.

Your job during that phone call is to *listen* to your customer. Those who listen build better relationships, know more about customer needs, and close more business.

Inability to See Customer Reactions. On the phone, we have to determine where our customers are in their thinking with only their words and the tone in their voice to go by. There are many messages in the nonverbal part of communication that can give us a direct line to a close:

- Does the customer sound hurried?
- Are there hesitations in the customer's comments?
- Are you hearing enthusiasm and fast tempo?
- Does the customer sound friendly and engaged, or irritated at having been interrupted?

What information can you gather about customers from the *way* they speak? A great deal can be learned from tone and tempo, but you need to listen purposefully beyond the words themselves. For example:

- "I am not the decision maker." (They probably want to get you off the phone, but they likely know who is making the decision.)
- "You've caught me at a bad time." (If said quickly and in a friendly way, they may be interested but it truly *is* a bad time. Ask for an appointment.)

Listen to yourself as you read aloud each statement below. Be sure to note the different meanings conveyed when you emphasize a different word.

- "We are not *really* purchasing at this time." (Hmmm, maybe they are thinking about putting it out for bids? How do you get on the bid list?)
- "We are *not* really purchasing at this time." (When might this customer want to purchase? Ask about a time frame, or a changed initiative.)
- "We are not really *purchasing* at this time." (Is this a lease or outsource opportunity?)
- "We are not really purchasing *at this time*." (Once again, what is the customer's time frame. Ask about contract deadlines or fiscal year, or schedule an appointment for a later date.)

Solution: Use the personality types as a template. Once you've determined what type your customer is, you will be able to compare what you are hearing on the phone to the predictable behavior of that type.

Then picture the customer; try to imagine a live person. Summon up an image of age, hair color, expressions they might have, and even their work environment. Are they standing on a factory floor wearing a hard hat? Is this an executive in a glass-walled office? Use the personality types to help you picture the person on the other end of the line. This will help you stay tuned in.

Short Attention Span. Many people in sales tend to be right-brain dominant and, quite frankly, often a little on the high-energy side. These are great assets in our business, but they can cause us to have a short attention span for ideas coming in from the outside. We get bored during the call when the customer is talking, especially if he or she is rambling.

This really isn't surprising, considering that people talk at only about 250 words per minute, and the brain can process at more than 1,000 words per minute (look at speed-readers). Eventually, our high-speed brains drive us to start looking around for something entertaining. Unfortunately, when we do that, we become redirected. Mentally zoning out can cause us to miss an important element in the conversation, an element that might determine the sale.

Solution: Instead of "zoning out," try the following:

Take notes. Write down what the customer is saying. Capturing a customer's keywords is an important way to track what he or she is thinking. Writing is a good way to keep you focused, and the notes are helpful long after you have finished the call. Plus, you now have a written record of the conversation that you can refer to later, enter into your contact manager, and use for preparing a customer-centered proposal. (Note that writing is more effective for retention than typing, because of how the brain processes information.)

Recap during the conversation. Active listening is so rare in business conversation that when you can accurately rephrase what the customer has said, the surprise value alone may get the customer's attention.

Doodle. This engages your brain by supporting the hands to brain connection.

Play with a squeeze ball. Use your left hand to engage your right brain. Or vice versa—whole-brain thinking will allow you to be sharper and better able to remember what is being said.

Walk around your space. You may be someone who thinks better when you are moving.

> **TALK TIP**
>
> Try this when you are on your next call. Put a pen and pad by the phone. During the conversation, every time you recognize that you have drifted away from your customer focus, put a mark on the pad. At the end of the call, note how many marks you have and make a mental note to try for fewer the next time. You may be surprised how often you have gotten off track when you thought you were generally paying attention. Keep practicing until you can stay with the customer for seven full minutes at a time.

ATTITUDE CHALLENGES

One important aspect of our willingness to listen is the value we place on time; another is the value we place on what the customer has to say relative to what we want to say. These two factors are attitude issues and are dealt with next.

Impatience. Because most salespeople have been through lots of product training, we are often eager to spill out all we know in a sales call, especially when we are aware that time is short. However, in most sales calls your job is to move the process along to advance the sale, and that means patiently hearing as much as the customer offers in order to better connect when it's time to close the deal. So the bottom line is to listen and take notes whenever the customer is talking.

Those of us with really high-speed thinking may be less aware of exactly how much time has passed during our conversations with customers. As long as the customer is talking, your chances of getting the sale go up. The reverse is true as well. As long as you are talking, the customer's interest is probably down. Although one of our greatest assets as sales professionals is our willingness to communicate, sadly, one of our detriments is that we tend to talk too much.

Solution: Use the tongue trick. When you are tempted to interrupt, take your tongue and place it behind your teeth. This acts as a gentle physical reminder to be quiet until the customer is finished. (You can use this technique in face-to-face interactions as well, and no one is the wiser.) This will help you to abide by our 80/20 rule: The customer should be talking 80 percent of the time. While the customer is talking, be sure that you are *actively listening*, rather than waiting for your turn to talk. Remember: You should be speaking only 20 percent of the time. So, given this guideline, *do you* talk too much?

You have probably not timed yourself to see if you are adhering to the 80/20 rule. It might be worth your while to time a few of your calls, to see whether you or your customer is doing most of the talking.

This rule is especially effective in dealing with **E**s and **A**s, who really want to run the conversation. **P**s and **K**s are better listeners, so you may alter those proportions for them, but be careful. Often, **P** and **K** salespeople feel the need to provide too many details in the conversation, risking a lost customer at the other end of the phone line.

Lack of Interest in Other People. Another attitude element is our own lack of interest in others. Ouch! Be truthful now; if customers on the other end are boring or don't talk openly, you may feel the need to talk more to keep the conversation going. Resist that urge, even though you think that what you have to say is *much* more interesting than what they have to say! Instead, figure out why they are boring. This could be because you have not asked enough pertinent questions. The customer may have even said "no" earlier, and because you didn't listen and kept going, he or she has now zoned out, is multitasking, or is just waiting for a pause to break in and hang up.

Some of us are genuinely curious about our customers and their individual stories. Others see people as merely a means to an end. Whatever your own basic attitude is, it probably comes through in your phone manner.

Solution: Use personality-matching to make phone interaction more interesting. A prospect becomes a puzzle that you solve by uncovering clues within conversations that you engineer. It is *your* job to find what is interesting about them. Take the three most boring customers or prospects you have and apply the personality-matching techniques to your next conversation. You might find that the issue is a personality-type difference between you two. When that's the case, by using the strategies in this book, you can turn boredom into bucks!

> ### A Greener Way to Do Business
> How much CO_2 is used when you travel to see a customer to deliver a presentation? From Atlanta to San Francisco, 1.5568 tons of carbon is used just for you. This is an emissions cost of $39.46. Staying at hotels just twelve nights per year uses 1.9237 tons of carbon with a CO_2 cost of $48.77.   *Source: travelgreen.org*

Listen While Presenting: I-N-V-O-L-V-E Your Customer

Since good listening can be exhausting, actively hearing and processing information while strategizing the next level of the conversation takes a lot of energy. For this reason, occasional breaks in your call day will help. What should help more, though, is remembering that the *reason* for listening is for you to *make the sale* to anyone over the phone. Combining good listening with strategic presenting will take you to the close more quickly.

Today's customers have about a thirteen-second attention span. What to do? Keep the customer involved. It is especially important in phone selling to get the customer involved right from the start.

Here are the steps you need to take for ensuring that the customer is indeed listening, paying attention, *and* thinking of buying from you. The acronym INVOLVE will help you remember what to do.

I—*INTEREST your customer.* Try something that your competition has never tried before. Do something different to help create excitement and to establish your creativity as a professional during your presentation. Have some fun with it; your customer will, too! Use these enhancements:

- A colorful story.
- A satisfied customer you can conference in for a testimonial.
- A product comparison that you can email during the conversation.
- A website you can refer the customer to while you are talking.

N—*NEVER use the phrase "I think" during your presentation.* Why? Because as a salesperson, your opinions are suspect since customers assume you are on commission. In addition, customers don't really care about what *you* think; they care about what *they* think. They also care about what other customers or experts who have used your product or service think. Testimonials, review articles, and awards can all build your case. Make sure they're easily accessible in an online location or digital file for instant use. You may be tempted to use "I think" with **Kind** customers in particular to speed up their slow and reluctant decision style. Resist the urge. What's important is getting the *customer* to say: "I think we'll accept your proposal."

V—*VERBALLY keep the customer engaged by asking questions during your phone presentation.* For example, ask: "What do you think of that idea?" and "How much do you think that will save you in the long run?" or "Where can you use this?" Remember to pause and wait for the customer to answer after you have asked the question and take notes on the response.

O—*ORGANIZE your thoughts before presenting over the phone.* Remember today's customers and their very short attention spans? Be succinct, focus on this particular customer's specific needs, and don't talk too much. The better organized you are, the less chance you'll talk yourself right out of a sale! Customers remember in threes, so organize to focus on three specific selling points—and jot these down before you start your call. You can open with, "Ms. Solumba, there are three main features you might find interesting in your situation." Then go through the three features, keeping the information very brief.

L—*LET your customer interrupt.* If your customer is either excited or bored, you may be interrupted. If the customer is excited, great! Close the sale right there. If the customer is bored, they are telling you to move on to another point— that the one you're spending too much time on has lost their interest and isn't important to them. You can encourage interruption (and make sure the customer is paying attention) with the occasional pause. Pauses can be very powerful tools on the phone. In Western culture we rarely pause during conversation, so even a short, one- or two-second pause breaks the monotony of your presentation and gets the attention of your customer.

V—*VERIFY that what you are presenting are, in fact, the right ideas to suit your customer's most pressing needs.* How do you do this? By listening. Did the customer agree, interrupt, or cut you off? Listen for the clues and follow through with some ideas of your own. Remember to write down what the customer is saying in their own words throughout your call. When you go for the close, the more closely you sum up in the customer's words, the more in sync you'll sound. This will solidify the customer's confidence that he or she has made the right decision.

E—*EXPRESS yourself skillfully.* If you are emphasizing how your service worked with another customer, tell a story to make it interesting and compelling to the customer. If you focus on your customer's real need, you avoid rambling and establish your credibility. You'll find that the sale is just around the corner.

> **TALK TIP**
> Remember that you can't see boredom or excitement over the phone, so you need to listen carefully to the customer's tone and pause frequently to pull the customer's comments into the conversation.

Vary the Tools You Use for Effective Presentations

Of course you've been taught (or have picked up on your own) a method for presenting your product or service. Unfortunately, many of the methods that are so commonly used have become outdated and ineffective, especially when you use the same approach every time with every customer. Varying the format that you use to get across the advantages of your company's offerings can jump-start you toward a quicker close.

USE STORYTELLING

Customers respond to stories that give them past history or emphasize success. They remember stories that emphasize your product and how well that product has worked. If you sell heating and air-conditioning systems, and your systems are less expensive to maintain in the long term than your competition's, tell a story about a customer who saved 20 percent in maintenance costs over a five-year period. Keep it short and to the point.

Rules for stories that provide your customer with proof include the following:

- It must be authentic, because your customer may ask for more information or a reference.
- It must be short, no more than two to three sentences.
- It should establish your credibility and compliment your customer.
- It should not directly address your competitor's weaknesses or flaws.

- It must be practiced to ensure smooth and effective delivery.

The implication in stories is, "Customer, you are smart like our other smart customers, so you will want to use our product in just the same way."

We refer to this as providing a third-party testimonial, which is more effective than offering your opinion over the phone. You are now simply (yet importantly) the messenger for a positive experience another customer has enjoyed by conducting business with you.

Customers are much better informed today than they used to be. Buyers are more sophisticated these days because of the easy availability of information (just look at how much you can learn about products on the Web). You're not going to put anything past the customer, so go instead for a story you know or an experience with which you are familiar.

DROP NAMES

It is important to know when to name-drop to help you close more sales. If you are talking to a customer at a smaller company, compare other customers that are approximately the same size, provided they're not direct competitors. When you are talking with a Fortune 100 company, name-drop other 100s or 500s that are similar; they may be in the same industry but again, not direct competitors. For example, a frozen food distributor and a canned food distributor are the same industry, and may even have some of the same customers; however, they are not competing directly.

If there is someone your customer knows and likes, this is an excellent name to drop. For example, if you are selling help desk services to a company, you might use the internal contact's name with which you are already doing business. You need to know in advance that the two people like each other. If you don't have this information, however, you run the risk of using a negative association and possibly losing the sale.

Never use name-dropping when:

- What you sell is too confidential or if the situation requires extreme discretion.

- The name is the customer's direct competitor.
- The company's name or product may be offensive or insulting in your customer's eyes.
- The products are too different or unrelated (like pet foods and airplane parts.

AVOID STEAMROLLING

As salespeople representing products or services we believe in, we sometimes get wrapped around our knowledge. We are so excited about what we sell and so intent on what we want to say, that we feel like we have to throw out every neat feature and include a cherry on top! Let's face it, we begin to enjoy our captive audience because we all like people to listen to us.

For example, a sales rep who has just come through a lengthy new product training course would want to share his or her knowledge, especially if it is truly a super innovation. Any good salesperson is a subject matter expert, and it makes sense that you are eager to convey all you've learned. Unfortunately, the customer may need only a tiny piece of what you know. The customer *only* wants his or her problem solved—not an encyclopedia of *all* you know.

Now, ask yourself this tough question: Is talking more helping you close more sales? If you answer "yes," you are in the minority or you're deluding yourself.

Consider that when you talk longer than thirty seconds at a stretch, customers think you have talked too much—*unless* you are specifically addressing their needs, which you will discover only by *listening*!

Put a silent timer near the phone. (One of those minute timers that looks like a small hourglass is great.) Just for fun, time your customer as he or she talks. Then time yourself and let the timer help you regulate your talk time. When the sand runs low while you are talking, stop and ask the customer a check-in question, such as: "How does that sound to you, Fred?" or a even a closing question, such as: "Can you tell me your thoughts on that feature for your business?"

The Payoff

Presenting that comes before questioning and listening is the ultimate turnoff for customers. But a salesperson who listens can present strategically, engaging the customer with only what is important to the decision. These phone sales professionals sell more!

If Matt, the carpet salesman from the start of this chapter, has learned anything, his calls should go better. Let's listen in:

CUSTOMER: Just give me the bottom line.

MATT: Thanks for helping cut this process short. Because we have three different alternatives that might fit, if you give me a couple more pieces of information, I can narrow it down to exactly how to price this job.

CUSTOMER: Sure. So many of you guys want to suck up my time reading me the whole product manual. Go ahead.

So far so good. Here's another:

CUSTOMER: We all participate in the decision.

MATT: Great, tell me how the process takes place and who is involved.

CUSTOMER: Well, Andrew in HR and Keira in Accounting are a part of the group, but mostly it's LaVonne and Steven. By the way, I think the next meeting is Tuesday.

That was better! But let's see how else Matt might handle the call:

CUSTOMER: We'll probably be staying with Good Services Company until the end of the year.

MATT: Okay, can you tell me about what they're providing and how the contracts are awarded?

CUSTOMER: What I've seen is that they're just installers and handle any warranty issues. I really think that we should have one company for the carpet itself as well as the installation, but then, that's just my opinion.

MATT: Sounds good to me. That's what we do. Thanks for your help. How should we proceed to get information on that bid list?

Looks like Matt is on his way to a bonus year!

CHAPTER 7

Selling Through Objections

PHONE SALES CHALLENGE *– Nathan, who sells exercise equipment, expressed this difficulty: "The presentation is a piece of cake for me; I breeze right through it. But then, just when I think I've really nailed the sale, customers come up with some off-the-wall objections that throw me."*

In every salesperson's day, there is that moment of celebration. Sometimes it's a quiet moment, when you first recognize the customer is indeed going to buy. Sometimes it's loud cheering and doing the happy dance around your office after you've hung up the phone from closing a career-defining sale. Whichever you are experiencing, the process that took you there probably went much like a well-crafted symphony.

When there is a sour note in the "sales symphony," though, most salespeople agree that it's the objection part. And let's face it, *every* sales interaction includes some type of objection before the sale is complete. While objections can be valuable in moving the customer to a close, each objection has to be handled strategically and with skill. What follows are some examples of what happens when they are not.

The objection below concerns the initial call itself, before any opportunity for questioning or presentation occurs:

CUSTOMER: Thank you, but we're all set with computer equipment.

SALESPERSON: Well, thanks anyway. Bye.

In this scenario, the salesperson quit before asking any questions that might gain her information that would lead to a future sale. She didn't deal with the objection in the next call any better:

CUSTOMER: I really don't have time to talk with you.

SALESPERSON: Okay, I'll call you back later.

Call when? Call why? Again, she had no gain from this call. If you want to be successful, consider that every call *must* end in some kind of close—a step toward a sale. Below is an example of how another salesperson dealt poorly with a common evasion:

CUSTOMER: Just send me some information.

SALESPERSON: Great! I'll get that in the mail to you and follow up later.

This call at least set up a reason for a follow-up, but it didn't nail down any specifics. The word "information" is pretty general, too general to give the salesperson any way to know what to send. Or, for that matter there isn't any setup in the customer's mind for a reason to look at the information when it arrives. So, first, the salesperson may be wondering how much information to send, and second, the customer is probably just telling the sales rep to "send it" to get him off the phone quickly. In short, this is a wasted call.

A "quick question" strategy would have helped here: "If I can ask you just two quick questions, I will know exactly what to send you." This strategy is easy, short, and powerful in helping you to get past this call objection.

Objections to specifics of the product, delivery, implementation, and the like, are also often handled poorly,

CUSTOMER: Your price is way out of line.

SALESPERSON: I can't see why you're complaining about our prices. We just had a price decrease that makes us the most competitive company in the industry.

This is a case of arguing with the customer, which is never a good plan. This may be the fifth time you've heard that objection today, and you're really tired of it, but that's a professional discipline problem. Arguing is not only ridiculous, it closes all doors for any future contact or sales.

Of course it can be exhausting dealing with the same objections over and over. And regardless of what is being sold, price seems to always come in as one of the most commonly heard objections. However, the customer has no idea how your day has gone, and you should never react as if anyone else thinks your prices are too high. Reacting defensively is not handling the objection. Plus, how do you even know if the objection is valid? Price is an easy play on the customer's part. You need to find out what the real problem is. Here's another example of what not to say:

CUSTOMER: We really are satisfied with our current supplier.

SALESPERSON: Well, is it okay if we call back in a couple weeks to check back with you?

This is a classic error. Why is the salesperson calling back? Why would anything be different in a couple of weeks? Customers don't make decisions based on a two-week time frame. They can make decisions tomorrow, next week, or two months from now. At the very least, if you were the salesperson in this situation, you should find out what the process is for selection, what the customer likes (and doesn't like) about the current supplier, and when changes *are* possible.

Instead of frustrating you (as in the above examples), objections can become an easy part of your phone call because rarely are they unique. You've heard many of them before and should be prepared for them. In addition they can be very valuable steps to a close.

The Value of Objections

The *real* value of hearing objections is that the customer is telling you that he or she is still paying attention and involved in the call, and that you still have the opportunity to make a sale. If the customer is *not* asking questions or objecting, he or she has mentally checked out. And as you know, when the customer checks out, your sale is *dead*. If you think of an objection not as an obstacle, but as a hurdle that must be navigated before moving on, you come closer to winning.

If you listen closely, there are clues that will tell you if your customer has mentally checked out of the call:

- You hear the customer's keyboard chatter in the background.
- The customer sounds like his or her head is down, voice muffled.
- You ask, "How does that sound to you?" and the customer says "uhm" or "uh" or "I'm not sure."
- The customer pauses too long after you ask a question.
- The customer says something like, "OK, well, I've heard all I need to hear."

Any of these situations say that the customer wasn't listening. When this happens, you need to be able to stimulate the customer's interest by asking a question. In an ideal world, customers pay full attention, focus completely on your presentation, and say, "Sounds good to me; let's close the deal." But this isn't an ideal world, and rarely is a sales call that simple. Note the caller/customer interaction below:

SALESPERSON: Are you ready to take delivery?

CUSTOMER: I'm not going to do something that quickly unless you agree to handle shipping charges.

The customer's response indicates that she is ready to buy or to negotiate. It's a signal that value is established, and that the details just need to be worked out.

Still not quite ready to say "hooray" when the customer objects? Is it fear that the customer will ask you something you don't know the answer to? Are you afraid he will attack you on behalf of your company for some past error? Do you worry that he might know more than you do? Well, as the song says, "don't worry, be happy": the tips you will learn here will help you turn worrying (and whining!) into *winning*.

There are three things (see, we take our own advice) to keep in mind when faced with customer objections. First, in phone sales you have a big advantage. You are invisible. This means that:

- You can have a written cheat sheet available to assist you with the tough ones.
- The customer cannot see any signs that you are nervous—perspiring, fidgeting, etc.
- You can formulate a strategic response more easily, because you aren't looking directly into a customer's eyes.
- You are not being distracted by the customer's environment.

Second, remember that you are on the phone and that although the customer can't see you, he or she can hear you. You must always *sound* calm, cool, and collected, with a relaxed and professional tone. If you do become uncomfortable, the customer won't have a clue—*if* you control your voice. To better prepare, here are some tips:

- Massage your neck to loosen tight vocal cords.
- Take a slow, deep breath to reduce your heart rate.
- Slow your rate of speech slightly, so you do not give the impression of being stressed or rushed.
- Stand up at your desk to open up your chest, allowing you to send plenty of air over your vocal cords for the clearest sound quality over the phone. (Sitting hunched at a desk restricts breathing and blood flow.)

Finally, the best way to not appear uneasy about an objection is to actually become comfortable with hearing objections. You have to be ready to respond, which is what gives you the advantage in a phone-selling situation. When you are *prepared*, it is *you* who commands the situation. When you come to the table knowing your customer's situation, your product, your competitors, and the usual objections, you have armed yourself with knowledge. And knowledge is not only power; it is also confidence. The goal is to avoid the unknown, which puts you on edge. You want to be able to move objections into the "known" column, and make them yet another part of the sales process over which you have control.

If you are able to anticipate any objections that you regularly hear, as well as any you can brainstorm and think of yourself, you'll be amazed at how much smoother you'll sound during the objection-handling portion of your calls. The result? More closed sales.

> **TALK TIP**
> It is not enough to do a one-time-only record of objections you hear. Regularly (at least once a month), study your list of objections and take time to think of new and truly strategic responses. Constantly update by adding any new information about your products or services, as well as your competition, to improve your answers. Practice with a coworker until you feel confident that you are on the right track to handle anything thrown at you.

Techniques for Handling Objections

Just as you don't have one outfit in your closet that takes you from a funeral to a ball game, you need a variety of techniques to handle objections capably. What follows are some of the approaches that you have at your disposal.

THE FIVE-STEP TECHNIQUE

You will find the five-step technique particularly useful to help you stay organized and clear as you answer the customer's objection. It involves careful listening on your part, but is extremely effective for setting up the close.

Step 1. When you first hear an objection, be quiet until the customer has completed the entire objection. Do not interrupt! (Remember the tongue trick?) It might help you to keep quiet if you jot down what the customer is saying to ensure you have a record of it. This will let you effectively counter all issues uncovered. This is especially important if you have a customer who asks highly technical questions that can be potentially complicated to answer, or if the customer isn't a clear communicator.

Step 2. Pause at the end of the objection (count to two). This pause says to the customer that you are thinking about the question or objection and that it is important to you. This also gives you time to clarify in your own head what you think you just heard and formulate your response. And it ensures that you are in control whenever you speak. You've probably heard the objection time and time again, but if you haven't, you've just provided yourself with the opportunity to think over a solution.

Step 3. Calmly and coolly handle the objection with your well-thought-out response. Be sure you handled *all* the concerns from Step 1. (That's why you wrote them down.) How did this person word the objection? Did you not add enough value in your presentation portion of the call? Do you know your customer and, if so, does this person generally object? Does the objection sound like a smokescreen (a false objection)?

Step 4. Go for a confirmation that the objection has truly been countered. After you feel you have satisfied the objection, ask the customer if you have resolved it to his or her satisfaction. For example, you might say one of the following:

- "Mary, does that answer your question?"
- "Steve, how does that sound to you?"
- "Leonard, do you like that idea?"
- "Jackie, if I've answered your question, are you ready to sign the agreement?"

The reaction will let you know if you have *really* handled the objection. You might think your response was both brilliant and sufficient, but what matters is that the customer's concerns are eliminated. Check your ego when you conduct a customer check-in.

Step 5. If the objection is indeed handled, oftentimes this is the perfect time to close. Negotiation is an opportunity to sell more, and can come out of an objection. Close with a question or by outlining a confirmation. For example:

"Taylor, you agree that we have the full-service solution for your installation. Why don't we go ahead and schedule our team to come in?

> **TALK TIP**
>
> Just a piece of advice for those who still connect *objection* with *rejection*: never take any objection personally unless the customer actually says, "I like your company and your products; it's *you* I don't like." (And when was the last time *that* happened? It's usually not about *you.*).

THE QUESTION TECHNIQUE

Another approach frequently used in many sales situations is what we call "the Question Technique." Asking questions helps you to gather critically important information. Perhaps even more important, it enables you to direct your customer's line of thought. We refer to this as "leading your customer down the garden path." The technique is to question so skillfully that the customer draws his or her own conclusion to buy. For example:

CUSTOMER: We've used the same cleaning company in our offices for three years. We see no reason to change.

SALESPERSON: Oh (pause). James, you said you've been using the same company for three years; what initially prompted you to go with your current service when you made that decision?

You find out why they changed at that time. It could have been price, or perhaps the previous supplier went out of business, or maybe even theft was an issue. Simply listen without interrupting. Hear what James has to say. Remember to listen to the tone. There is most likely some useful information that you can gain from his response. You will better know where to go from there. For example:

SALESPERSON: Can you tell me what you like about their service?

CUSTOMER: They use environment-friendly chemicals.

SALESPERSON: How important is that to you?

CUSTOMER: It's very important to us in the way we do business.

Now you are in a conversation. If this aspect of James's service provider is very important, you come back with questions that uncover possible weaknesses related to that. Use a problem that you are aware of from your knowledge of your competitor's methods. For example, let's say you know the smell of vinegar that remains after cleaning can be offensive:

SALESPERSON: James, what does it smell like after a treatment?

CUSTOMER: Gosh, what did the office smell like last time? Oh, yeah, it was pretty awful. It smelled like my mother-in-law's broom closet.

You see, you didn't *tell* the customer that you know about the odor, even though you had that information. You, instead, let James discover it on his own through your skillful questioning. Don't tell . . . *ask*. Customers who draw conclusions on their own, while you happen to be on the phone with them, think they're pretty smart, and that your timing is excellent.

Customers who are *told* what the problems are can get defensive. For example, if you tell the customer that you know that the carpet stinks after the competitor leaves, the customer is most likely to respond "no, it doesn't" without even thinking. With the question approach, you can confirm the problem very easily over the phone by learning more about the customer's real needs.

Let's get back to our customer, James. Now you know that being environmentally friendly is important to him. In addition you have called attention to the unpleasant odor. Your next step is to ask:

SALESPERSON: James, what if you found a company that used environmentally safe products that didn't leave a residual smell?

That at least puts you back into the conversation, and may lead to the following:

CUSTOMER: Oh, I guess we could take a look at that. What do offices smell like after your service cleans them?

SALESPERSON: How about if we clean your office for free one time and we'll see?

CUSTOMER: Sounds like a good idea. When can you come by?

> ### A Greener Way to Do Business
>
> Consider how "green" it is to handle objections over the telephone. You can scroll through your database of responses right at your desk and save valuable time and paper.

THE EMPATHY TECHNIQUE

Yet a third method of handling objections is what was once referred to as the "feel, felt, found" system. We have reworked this idea to reflect a more up-to-date approach called "the Empathy Technique." This technique has been around professional selling for many years, and is especially useful with **Energized** and **Kind** customers. There's a reason it's had such a long shelf life—it works! Just remember to mix this technique with other objection-handling methods during the course of your call.

Often, the first objection you will encounter is a variation of "we're fine the way we are." This is what we refer to as "the inertia objection":

CUSTOMER: I'm happy with my current supplier.

> **SALESPERSON:** Martina, I can see why you might have strong loyalty, because other customers have *expressed* something similar in the past, and what they *found* was . . .

Your answer must be brief and include a specific benefit to the customer. Be careful not to use the word "but"; instead, use "and," so it doesn't sound like you are arguing with the customer. Remember that on the phone you can't soften what you say with an engaging facial expression, so your word choice becomes crucial. If you have tried the empathy technique before and found it a bit tough to deliver, try using different synonyms in the technique to sound more natural in your ears and the customer's:

> **SALESPERSON:** James, I can understand why you are telling me this. We've heard this from other office managers as well. And what they found was . . .

Or:

> **SALESPERSON:** . . . by simply trying our service on two occasions, customers found the carpet was not only cleaner, it was fresher smelling, too. What are your thoughts about that?

A mistake salespeople often make when they try to use this technique is that they talk too much during the benefit section of responding to the objection. Long spiels are too difficult for customers to follow on the other end of the phone. Less is more.

USING CONFIRMATION TO CHECK YOURSELF

Salespeople sometimes mistakenly think that if a response has covered an objection for them, it is covered for the customer as well. Not necessarily so. You need to ask the question for confirmation. Often the customer will not volunteer that he or she is satisfied and ready to buy. You must check with the customer every time you answer an objection, regardless of the technique you use in handling the objection. Here are some examples of check-ins:

- "How do you feel about that?"
- "Will that fly with the boss?"
- "What do you think about this idea?"

- "Will that work for you?"
- "How does that sound?"

Once you secure a solid confirmation, you can move right into the close:

SALESPERSON: If we can clean carpets using environmentally safe products, and do away with the odor that bothers you, will you give us a try?

Now that's a close that works!

GETTING ON TOP OF THE CALL

Experienced phone salespeople have to use every technique, method, and system they can think of, and lots of just plain common sense. Here are a few more suggestions to help you deal with customer objections.

Practice with Colleagues, a Recording Device, and Even with Customers. Yes, even with customers! Learn what works. It is a mistake to simply write down or silently read over a list of potential objections and their counters. You will be much more relaxed and effective if you practice saying your responses aloud. This sets up the recall system in your brain, so you don't suffer from "test" anxiety. Objections feel like a test to us, just like when we were in school. And we can't afford to have our mind go blank when we face objections. If you anticipate questions, know the answers, and practice recalling *and saying* them, you'll find that you can handle objections skillfully.

> **TALK TIP**
>
> For those of you who still feel that you may get a bit stressed when customers object, the following technique can help you to stay calm and in control. Just as remembering to bring insect repellent on the camping trip can prevent the discomfort of battling mosquitoes, preparing for objections can lessen stress considerably. Play through every scenario of objections you (or your friends or other sales team members) can think of. Most anything that you can expect, you can plan for. You're less likely to be blindsided if you've done a good job of anticipating.

Make a Practice of Pausing. Avoid rushing into a response to any objection. Give yourself a few seconds to think about the exchange. Take a moment to consider the customer's perspective. Think about what may be on her mind. If she has previously bought a product that was too slow in delivery, proved to be faulty, or was overpriced, then that customer, who may be accountable to others, may fear making another buying mistake, especially purchasing from a salesperson over the phone. Her objections may not be to *your* product. Perhaps you can uncover what's really going on for her. Addressing her *real* problem can only help you make the sale.

Take Every Objection Seriously. No matter how ridiculous you might think an objection is, or even if you think it is a smokescreen (a false objection to get rid of you), for the customer it may truly be a concern. Your professional and direct manner of handling it may earn you serious credibility points and more closed sales down the road.

Clear the Smoke. Speaking of smokescreens, they come in many forms. Your customer might feel obligated to object, or put up a barrier, even if there is no real concern. After all, a customer doesn't want you to feel like he or she is easy prey. Remember, if you haven't established value for the specific customer you're talking with, price is irrelevant. So a price objection can be a smokescreen for something else altogether. Also, if a customer doesn't want to do something, one reason is as good as another. Use questioning to see through the smoke so you can address the real objection.

Use Personality-Matching Strategies. As soon as you determine the personality type you are dealing with (**P, E, A,** or **K**), many techniques for managing that person's objections can come to your aid. Plan and prepare for handling customer objections before making the closing phone call. Having a strategy in place will not only relieve your anxiety, but can also make the difference between a brush-off and a closed sale.

Personality-Type Objection Patterns

In the paragraphs that follow are guidelines concerning what kinds of objections you might expect from each personality type. You will find handling those objections easier than you might have thought.

THE PRECISE CUSTOMER

Precise people, because they are cautious, have the most objections, both in number and obscurity. Be prepared for the **Precise Customer** with information to back up your responses. A **P** customer will sound skeptical, detailed-oriented, and even nitpicky to your ears. The more technical **P** customer will go for the details. If your equipment has a 0.1 percent failure rate, the **Precise** will say, "What if we get the product that is defective?"

This customer might "what if" you to death. (Patience is a virtue!) Perhaps it's your perception that they are just putting up a smokescreen, but their real concern is that every contingency be covered. So you must handle each objection precisely, accurately, and honestly.

To handle **P**s, keep your emotions in check. Use facts to respond to objections. Offer proof in the form of white papers, third-party testimonials from objective sources (such as trade reviews), expert testimony, spec sheets, failure/success rates, anything you can use to demonstrate the proof. Email an article or send the customer to a website while you are still on the phone and discuss the proof document at that moment. After all, these are the most critical customers and they don't generally buy into a salesperson's suggestions immediately.

THE ENERGIZED CUSTOMER

Energized Customers are sloppy with their objections. The poorest of listeners, their objections will sound emotional, yet assertive and quick, and maybe even too hasty and not clearly thought out. In addition, they will attempt to retain the relationship even during the objections with phrases like, "Please, don't take this personally," or "I'm sure you're the top of your field, but we can only afford the middle. You're going to have to give me a break."

An **E** may try to persuade you to make special allowances: "You know we've been doing business with your company for a long time. Doesn't that afford us an extra deal once in a while?"

To handle an **E** customer, keep your own enthusiasm up. Emphasize value. Demonstrate how your service will make the decision maker look good, personally. Use humor to counter the **E**'s objection, but don't use it in a sarcastic, offensive way. Humor should be something you can both laugh at, to assist in building rapport.

THE ASSURED CUSTOMER

Assured Customers will get right to the point with objections, sometimes phrased almost as a challenge. They may just object for the fun of it because they like to win and will negotiate as sport. The actual wording of the objection might sound mean over the phone, but remember, it's a game to them. Because an **A** is abrupt, you will hear the objections briefly and assertively pronounced. For example, an **A** might say, "Keenan, your price is just way out of line." The **A** does not sugarcoat the message: "Can't afford you" or "Nope, won't work."

You need to recognize what is really happening; an **A** *has* to negotiate. As sound unmoving and are generally motivated by feeling that they've won. (And if an **A** doesn't feel like he or she has won, you've lost the deal. Period.)

If you are an **A** yourself, this would be stimulating, because you enjoy a challenge, too. If you are a **Kind**, though, it might be very stressful to deal with this type. Resist the urge to take the **A**'s objection personally. It's not about *you*.

To **Assured Customers** you should sound very confident; do not flounder, waffle, or hesitate. Answer factually; don't get emotional. Tie your response to the needs and objectives you know that the customer has, and then add value for the **A**. If you are selling carpet cleaning, and the **A** customer says, "Why should I pay $500 per office when I can get it done for $300?" respond with: "Because we use chemicals that are nontoxic, safely eliminating the stench that you find offensive. Not only that, we're faster than the competition because of state-of-the-art cleaning equipment, so you'll have less down time. You'll see the difference immediately." Pause. Then ask, "What do you think of that?"

Sometimes you can even challenge them back right on the phone: "The last time you had your offices cleaned by the lowest bidder, what kind of results did you get?"

As long as you are still involved in a conversation with the customer, you have a chance of closing the business. Keep the exchange two-way with questions that will help you to add value to the transaction.

THE KIND CUSTOMER

Kind Customers do not want to hurt feelings, and sometimes this makes them harder to deal with, especially in phone conversations, since they prefer face-to-face interactions. A **K** dislikes telling you no. Hidden objections often are not related to the voiced objection. If you could physically see a **Kind** objecting, you would immediately notice the physical cues of squirming and avoiding eye contact, but over the phone, you will have to listen carefully for verbal phrasing to clue you in.

Objections a **K** might use include the following:

- "I don't know if I can get this past my boss."
- "It sounds good, but we just had our carpets cleaned not too long ago."
- "We really don't want to rush into making a decision."
- "We'll just have to review the options as a team."

The hidden objection might be any number of things. The price is off, the customer doesn't like your manner, or this **K** really *isn't* the decision maker. Putting you off is easier for a **K** than directing you to the real point of resistance. It's possible that there is no intention or desire to change, but the **K** still wants to be nice to you. You may even hear distress in the **K**'s voice on the phone. Also, keep in mind that the **K** is a slow, cautious decision maker. It takes longer to close this customer, so you may just need to work on him or her over a longer period of time to secure the business.

At some point, you need to uncover the true objection without challenging this person. If you get a lot of "maybe" or "yes" answers but the customer will not close or ask for follow-up calls, this is probably a **Kind** who has decided no, but doesn't want to hurt your feelings. You have to then decide whether it's worth pursuing based on the time-sensitivity of your situation.

To handle a **Kind** customer, empathize and make the deal as personal as possible by using your most gentle—yet confident—tone. Also, get the **K**'s coworkers involved. **K**s like to bring in their team so the responsibility of the decision isn't left entirely up to them.

> **Salesperson:** Mary, I can see where this decision might put you in a tight situation, since you've had a relationship with your current supplier. Let's see how we can make this easier for you and your office staff to make a transition.

The Payoff

Whether you are responding with one of the objection-handling techniques discussed earlier in the chapter, or are beginning to incorporate personality types into your strategy, your perception of objections can affect the entire sales call. Remember that objections are just hurdles, not walls. Expect objections *every time*, so handling them is not a big deal. Doing this is part of sharpening your sales performance skills.

The more effective you become at handling objections, the more effective you will be in your selling career, regardless of what you sell. Remember, handling objections effectively is a *learned* skill. No one is born an expert at handling objections, so the more you study and practice, the better you will be. Ready? Set? Go!

Now it's time to check in on Nathan to see if he's practicing the new skills:

> **CUSTOMER:** We're all set with our current equipment supplier.

> **NATHAN:** Do you mind if I ask you a few quick questions about your in-use times?

Good job, Nathan! He pushed for some information. If he knows that the equipment they're currently using has poor performance, he'll be able to make some points. Now let's see the customer's attempts to brush him off:

> **CUSTOMER:** I really don't have time to talk to you.
>
> **NATHAN:** Okay, when might you have three minutes that I can ask you about your in-use rates on your exercise equipment?

This time he made it clear that he wasn't going to make a long feature-dump presentation. He will be able to gain the information, get off the phone, and set up the opportunity to talk again.

Let's see what happens when Nathan attempts to use the "quick questions" strategy.

> **CUSTOMER:** Just send me some information.
>
> **NATHAN:** I'm happy to do that and because we handle both free-weight and tension-resistance equipment, I need to ask a few quick questions to send you exactly what would interest you.

Now that was slick! He got in what they offer and asked for some information. Now, though, we get to observe the tough, features-specific objections:

> **CUSTOMER:** Your price is way out of line.
>
> **NATHAN:** Well, tell me more about your pricing expectations.

And another:

> **CUSTOMER:** We're really satisfied with the equipment we have leased.
>
> **NATHAN:** Oh? Tell me about how that works for you guys.

And finally:

> **CUSTOMER:** I just don't see us adding recumbent bicycles when we already have uprights.
>
> **NATHAN:** I can see where you might think that and I've had customers before who thought that way. They found, though, that doctors are starting to recommend recumbents specifically for their lack of stress on the back.

All right! That's the way to blast those objections!

CHAPTER 8

Negotiating the Close

PHONE SALES CHALLENGE – *Mandy, who sells corporate meeting services for an upscale resort in the mountains of western Colorado, had this question: "I lost a huge sale with a national account. My boss said that I oversold, missed the close signal, and blew the sale. How can you oversell?"*

You will not have the customer "with you" at the close unless you have been "with" him or her during your entire call. As long as you are talking away, rattling off a list of benefits or awards your company has won, you are not guiding the sales conversation. You may, in fact, be delivering a solo performance to an audience that has already left the room! Unless you keep your customer involved by asking questions throughout the sales conversation, you won't know what hot buttons to home in on. Also, news flash, the customer isn't going to interrupt your spirited oratory to say, "Excuse me, I'd like to buy now, so will you kindly *shut up*?"

The lack of two-way involvement makes the close for so many salespeople just a shot in the dark, an unsupported guess, with all the stress and uncertainty that guessing creates. Let's look at some examples of ineffective close statements and see where they led:

CUSTOMER: How soon could we get delivery?

SALESPERSON: Sarah, by the way, I just wanted you to know that before we take your order, we'll need to run a credit check on your firm. That's going to take about twenty-four hours.

CUSTOMER: You know, I don't really need to make that decision now. Never mind.

Hmmm. There's an unhappy outcome. When the customer gives you a close message, you close! You certainly don't throw obstacles in the way. This poor salesperson has just told the customer that her firm's credit is in doubt and that the sale is on hold for a full day. Now let's look at another close:

CUSTOMER: I really like your warranty plan as well as your three-day delivery. What would the cost be?

SALESPERSON: Darryl, I know cost is a concern for you. What do you want to spend?

Bad call! Instead of answering the customer's question and moving quickly toward the close, this salesperson has answered a question with a question. That can sound evasive and suggest that there might be a problem with the price.

The salesperson's question was also poorly phrased. "Spend" is a bad word to use with the customer. No one likes to feel they are spending, but that they are "investing" in a solution. Okay, let's look at one more example:

CUSTOMER: Yes, I can see where this might work well for us.

SALESPERSON: Great! Can you have a check ready for us this afternoon?

CUSTOMER: This afternoon? I'm afraid not. We'll just have to look at this later.

Depending on what is being sold, asking for a check *this* afternoon can be an acceptable request or it can be considered pushy. In this situation it was obvious that the customer had no idea that immediate payment would be required. Payment may not be a problem, but there could be approvals and procedures involved that would require more time before the check could be cut.

Again, this approach depends on the type of product or service you are selling. Getting the money is certainly the goal, but often the difference between closing a sale and *not* closing it is being aware of what your customers' procedures are for payment. Realistic requests can cement a close; requests that surprise or trouble a customer can shut it down. A better way may have been for the salesperson to explain to the customer that, "To secure an implementation date, we'll need a deposit of X amount by the twelfth. Will that work for you?" Or to say, "We'll need a deposit to get started on the project. When can we have it?"

Sales, as a profession, often attracts people who love the rush and high of the close, the final culmination of prospecting, planning, and managing the selling process. This is a good thing as long as the customer is left with the same excitement about the purchase decision after he or she is no longer on the phone with you, as long as the customer also feels satisfied with the transaction. The close does not have to be stressful or pressured; instead, it can be the natural result of a partnership between you and the customer that serves your goal (the purchase decision) and meets the customer's needs (a solution).

Set Up the Close

From the moment you plan to call a customer, you should have strategized how you are going to set up your close. But it is in the phone conversation itself that you can take steps to ensuring a positive outcome by using the **feature** → **benefit** → **check-in** process (F-B-C). The check-in process is the way you find out how the customer truly feels about what you have just said, and you learn the significance of each feature to the client. It is the part of your presentation that allows you to confirm the elements that will lead you to the close.

When using the F-B-C formula of presenting, visualize a club sandwich. You know, first a slice of bread, then some meat, a vegetable, then repeat. It's the same as when you are using the F-B-C process. The first slice of bread on top is the "feature." The meat is the "benefit," and the veggie is the "check-in." Then, another slice of bread, another feature, and continue until you have built yourself, and your customer, a delectable sandwich.

By using this process of presenting, you ensure that the customer stays involved in the call, you know what they want, and there isn't too much presenting, which can provide the customer with an opportunity to check out on the call.

AVOID DANGLING FEATURES

As a professional salesperson you know all about features and benefits, right? So you would never leave a dangling feature—mentioning a feature without immediately explaining its benefit—would you? Of course not. Salespeople who just throw out features (or benefits or specs) are not laying the proper groundwork for a close.

A feature is a fact, such as: "We have 24/7 customer service," or "Our company has won nine product excellence awards," or "We deliver to your doorstep within twenty-four hours." Any feature may represent a benefit to most of your customers. But since customers usually aren't listening as closely as we'd like on the other end of the phone, it's critical to follow your presentation of each feature with its specific benefit (or benefits) to this particular customer.

INCLUDE A BENEFIT STATEMENT

There are basically only five benefits in the business world, regardless of the good or service you are selling:

1. Saves time.

2. Saves money.

3. Increases revenue.

4. Reduces stress.

5. Improves productivity.

While there might be specifics related to the particular industry, such as reducing head count or handling waste, ultimately they can all be translated into one of these five benefits.

When presenting a feature to a customer, include a benefit statement and resist the urge to talk too much. It's easy for a customer to get lost and tune out.

Also, *every time* you mention a benefit to your customer, include a phrase such as: "And what this means to you is . . ." or "And the benefit to you is . . ." or "What you'll get out of this is . . ."

In selling to resellers, however, you have to use a two-layer approach for stating benefits. For example, if an original equipment manufacturer (OEM) makes cell phones for a cellular service company, the company has two levels of needs that must be satisfied. The first level of need is the direct operational cost saving of the item. If you are selling a scratchproof plastic for the cover of the cell phone, the benefit you offer is that it is both inexpensive and easy to fabricate. The OEM's second level of need is a market advantage, and the benefit you offer is that the scratchproof case is something the reseller's customers will appreciate.

A true sales pro will recognize and capitalize on the opportunity to meet a customer's two levels of need, thereby cementing the benefit advantages and making it easier for the customer to buy. To return to the example above, by building a bridge between the OEM's operational expense (a cost saving) and the end-user's advantage (a scratchproof case), you have set up an effective close.

CHECK IN WITH THE CUSTOMER

In face-to-face sales calls, you have the luxury of being able to read the nonverbal cues, to see what benefits have hit home. Over the phone, it may seem impossible to know what the customer is really thinking because you won't always get an audible reaction. The way to find out what the customer is thinking is to "check in" by asking questions *during* the presentation portion of your call and immediately *after* each small amount of information you provide. Checking in allows you to determine the customer's acceptance level, to learn how the customer truly feels about what you have just said, and to gauge the significance of that particular feature in the customer's mind. This interactive approach also keeps the customer with you during the call and makes it far less likely and far more difficult for him or her to drift away from the conversation.

You can check in with a customer using questions as simple and straightforward as:

- "How do you feel about that?"
- "When can you use this to your advantage?"
- "How important is that to you on a scale of one to ten?"

If the customer's response to the benefit is positive, you have a hot button to note (do jot it down). The customer's response might even signal an opportunity for you to close. The result of your check-in tells you what your next step should be. When you frame your presentation in this way, you set yourself up for success by eliminating objections while gaining interaction and buy-in.

If, on the other hand, the customer's answer to your question is negative, you have learned that the feature and benefit are not important to this particular customer. Then move on! Even if, in your experience, they are important to *all* other customers, your only concern should be the customer in *this* call. Work harder at uncovering matches, rather than dogging the issue to try to convince a customer. If you make the situation adversarial by hanging on, the result can be a lost sale.

Remember F-B-C: feature → benefit → check-in!
If you get all positives, you can go to a close at any time, often without any objections whatsoever.

Eliminate Buyer Anxiety

Whatever customers buy from you—whether it is computer equipment or maintenance products—they feel accountable for their purchase. If a buyer purchases a computer system that fails to perform up to standards or cleaning supplies that have an offensive odor, they fear some sort of reprisal for a bad decision: loss of respect, ridicule, or even a reprimand. That is part of the customers' price considerations—not just the dollar expense, but also the *professional* expense.

The professional salesperson understands the total cost that the customer is considering. This is:

total cost to customer = dollar investment + time + risk

In other words, by eliminating the buyer's anxiety, you ensure that there won't be excessive returns or afterthought cancellations, both of which cost you money in short-term business and, even more important, in long-term dollars. Using a process format to guide the sales cycle ensures that the sale will stick.

Overcoming the voiced objections is straightforward, but this perceived risk element is something you may have to surmise or uncover on your own. You won't be able to see a concerned expression on your prospect's face over the phone, so listen closely to the customer's tone and/or silence to help you strategize your next move.

ANTICIPATE PERSONALITY AND RISK

Taking into account your customer's personality style and perceived risk will give you clues to possible close opportunities. No matter how many hot buttons you hit or objections you overcome in the conversation, you still have to listen for stress points. Until those have subsided, *no sale!*

The Precise Customer. Since the **Precise Customer** is generally overly cautious, is fact-oriented, and avoids change, any lack of preparedness on your part or absence of data will cause this customer's risk meter to jump. **P**s are *extremely* risk averse, but often respected for their concern with informational detail. Although often not the final decision maker, the **P**'s input will be regarded with seriousness and can quickly kill a deal if negative. **Precise Customers** especially enjoy being perceived as the expert. Thus, making a mistake and losing the esteem of colleagues would be too high a price for a **P** to pay.

The phone is the perfect medium for handling **P**s because they are more interested in data than in knowing you anyway.

> *Risk-Management Strategy.* Make certain that the **P** has a load of data, such as product samples, white papers, demos, third-party testimonials, financial data, articles from trade journals, test results, and anything else you can provide when you make your call. If the **P** is convinced of your product's merit, he or she will sell for you to the decision maker. They will go about this by digging in their heels and swearing up and down that the decision they've researched is indeed, the *correct* one. In group decision-making meetings, **P**s are not necessarily the most popular, but their opinions are well respected.

The Energized Customer. The **Energized Customer** is emotional and can buy in the heat of the moment on impulse. So, at first glance, the **E** may seem to be a risk taker. The good news is that the **E** might change quickly from a competitor's service to yours. This can work for or against you; buyer's remorse is no stranger to the **E** because of this excited impulsivity.

Thus, the professional risk for the **E** is the potential to be thought foolish by the boss or coworkers. With jobs as precarious as they are these days, the **Energized Customer** may even fear losing a job if the decision is disastrously wrong. For this reason, **E**s may bring a coworker or second decision maker into the situation—generally someone with a different personality style. Buying because it "felt right" may have gotten your **E** customer into real trouble at some point in the past.

> *Risk-Management Strategy.* Get excited along with the **E**; let them hear it in your voice, and show them that their decision will make them look good. Deepen the relationship with regular follow-up contacts, so that you become a trusted partner. When a third party is brought in, you can likely assume that the **E** has already decided in your favor. So, when

you talk to this third party, it might be a good idea to have the **E**, whom you've already convinced, on a conference call. Your job will be to handle the other person and to reassure the **E** that the decision is a good one and that he or she will personally benefit.

Also, remember **Energized Customers** lose things, so always have an extra copy of the agreement in a brightly colored organizational folder to send as a follow-up to your call, and email messages with backup data in case you need to resend information and to assist this **E** in keeping track of your "stuff." With this customer, it's a good idea to always blind-copy yourself on anything you send—then it's right there to be sent out again if necessary. *Note:* This also gives you a legitimate excuse to make a call back to the **E** to ensure that he or she has received what you have sent. Use this call-back to reiterate the solidness of the product and to appeal to the **E**'s real motivator—*recognition*.

The Assured Customer. Since **Assured Customers** see themselves as innovators and risk takers, they may appear to have no buyer anxiety. Truly, they generally only fear being bested in a deal—a major blow to an **A**. An **A** who finds no room to negotiate will feel this is too confining and may walk away from a deal.

A customers, though, are often politically motivated in their organization. They may put you on speakerphone if someone important is in their office when you call. If their anxiety level is high, they may become arrogant on the phone, and you can hear that in the **A**'s voice. Just remember, the price of the sale for the **A** will include career impact as well. **Assured** decision makers may love conflict and negotiating with you, but probably would chafe at the possibility of a bad purchase costing them politically. So make them look good.

Risk-Management Strategy. Remind the **A** often that he or she is getting a great deal. Be prepared to negotiate and not necessarily have the upper hand. You may want to hold something back at the beginning of a negotiation in order to present it as a freebie later. When the **Assured Customer** makes a decision, it may be marked only with a terse "okay." Don't talk too much during the close, or you might cause the **A** to rethink the wisdom of the decision. He or she is ready to move on; you should be, too.

The Kind Customer. **Kind Customers** fear confrontation, negotiation, and risk. They would walk miles out of their way to avoid these if necessary. Discord and the prospect of someone's feelings being hurt by their actions are almost painful. They are anxious not to put anyone else in a difficult situation. They will buy a particular car just for its no-haggle policy. As young people, **K**s were very naive and trusting, but if they have been taken advantage of enough times, they will see every deal as risky. Sadly, they begin to doubt their judgment, and they fear making a mistake.

Because of this, the **K** customer, like the **E** customer, will probably bring in a partner or a committee as protective armor for the decision—generally a **P**, who will slow the process, or an **A**, who will act as a hard-nosed negotiator.

> *Risk-Management Strategy.* Slow down! You will have to earn the trust of the **K** unless you want all dealings with him or her to be group decisions. Remember to use your voice in a more supportive and soothing way, rather than in a crisp and direct style. Walk the **K** through the closing process to make it easier for him or her to buy.

> For example, say:

> "Larry, it sounds like our software is right for your application based on what you told me. I can show you how easily it can be implemented in your department."

Paint the picture of satisfaction and ease of transition after the sale. List all the steps:

> "First our systems designer will go over the compatibility issues; then we'll plan the installation, which we can do dur-

ing your regular shutdown; and, finally we'll do the training—at our expense. We'll have your team up and running
within six to eight weeks."

Show the **K** customer that the decision is a *safe* one. Explain and
demonstrate with a detailed plan, to prepare for alleviating any potential snags. Support them in their decision.

> **TALK TIP**
>
> Everything you say over the phone should be geared to advancing
> the sale. Working in tandem with your customers allows them to
> feel in command; they can *own* the decision. Ownership makes
> the purchase decision impregnable to the competition, and
> makes long-term repeat business easier.

Ask for the Business

Closing the business *requires* asking for the order. Customers by nature will not say, "I am choosing you for this project." They will, however, give you an invitation or a clue when they want you to ask for
the close. Remember, if you have qualified correctly and established
a good consultative relationship, you can close at any time during
the process. All you need is enough "yes" responses on your check-
ins. Listen for the tone of the "yes" response as well; make sure it's
a "yes" of assent, not just to get you off the phone.

When a customer says any of the following comments, go for
your close:

- "That sounds good."
- "I like the ideas that you're sharing."
- "Maybe we need a change."
- "This is the best solution I've seen so far."

You will still need to *ask* for the business, though, in order to get
it! So, you need to respond with one of the following statements:

- "It sounds like we have the solution for you. Are you ready to place the order?"
- "Based on what you've told me, we have a great match. Can we get started on the agreement?"
- "Sounds like you are ready to go. When do you want to take delivery?"
- "I like what you're telling me. What do you need from me to get going on the implementation?"

The customer may be ready to buy, but you can still expect the possibility of negotiating a few of the final details during the phone call.

> **TALK TIP**
>
> No doubt you have heard the advice: Go for a close three times. This mindless repetition irritates customers; stop doing it. Another classic to avoid is, "How can we gain your business?" Customers asked this question repeatedly during a sales conversation feel badgered and will shut you down in a hurry. Give up outmoded techniques and use responsive strategies, not worn-out clichés.

REENGAGING AFTER "NOT NOW"

When you meet resistance with a customer response like, "We're not really ready to do that now," you can reopen the conversation by directing the focus back on the customer with a follow-up question. Try something along the lines of,

> "Oh, then tell me your expectation for delivery of the new line to your distributor."

When the customer has explained how much pressure they are under—for instance, to meet their deadlines—you can then back into the close with,

> "In that case, it sounds as if to meet *your* (note voice emphasis here) deliverables target date, you'll have to have a new

system in place within the next thirty days. Does that make sense to you?"

By adopting this approach you have taken the heat off the customer's need to make a decision and fanned the flames of his or her own pressures, making your solution a relief. You have closed in a more natural and responsive way in the customer's mind so that your product or service is the perfect choice.

Negotiate: Carve Out the Details

The rush that a salesperson craves and relishes can occur prematurely. Doing the happy dance should be saved for the signature, the purchase order, or the delivery date agreement. A customer's "yes" often only means "I agree with you in principle—*if* we can work out the details." In business-to-business selling particularly, you can have two versions of a "sale." One is the instant sale, in which an immediate exchange (or verbal promise) of money with an equally instantaneous shipment of product or appointment for service occurs. The other is the contract sale, which will likely require an additional follow-up call after a proposal or contract is sent.

Any salesperson can likely tell a story about an agreement secured on the phone that somehow fell apart during the final contract process. Just a few basics about negotiating may help cement that sale.

First: Is it a negotiation? You might think you are negotiating details of a close, when actually you are still meeting objections. You may not discover there is any impediment to the sale until you mention faxing the contract, emailing the proposal, or setting the installation date. When you make the follow-up call after the contract or proposal is sent, then you may indeed be in a negotiation.

Think of it this way. You might agree wholeheartedly that a Porsche Cayenne would meet all your needs for comfort, drivability, and passenger-hauling utility. You may love the color and believe every advantage the salesperson pointed out and you agree 100 percent with the general superiority of Porsche workmanship and service. But when the salesperson begins to put everything on paper and you find that the car you want has to be shipped from Canada and will take three weeks, the financing interest rate is higher than you had anticipated, and your state taxes luxury cars at a higher rate, suddenly the entire situation looks different.

Negotiating on the phone, especially in complex selling situations, is best supported by follow-ups to ensure the sale. Buyer's remorse or even legitimate changes in circumstances can derail a close that has not been worked through completely.

Second: What are you really negotiating? If you are reasonably sure you are through with the objections, then you have to clarify what you're actually negotiating. If your company is in a position to offer flexibility on some of the details of the sale, a little "good news" (faster delivery date, extended service contract, or the like) could go a long way toward getting concessions from the customer on payment times or even a larger contract or order.

Be cautious here. In the push to pin down all the details, be very careful to promise only what you are sure you can deliver for any kind of exchange of value. Remember, what you are agreeing to will be in the contract. If the customer service end of the business (tech support, warranty service, etc.) truly can't do what you are offering, then you could be shooting yourself in the foot where future business is concerned. Be real!

Third: Ask for what you want. At our local pizza delivery location, the order takers are told not to offer any discounts unless asked, but if someone asks, discounts are routinely available. Asking is just as important for salespeople. When you are going over the proposal details, don't forget to propose!

If you have established the kind of credibility that a solid consultative salesperson sets up, you should be able to pose alternatives to the customer that will steer him or her in the direction you would choose. For example,

"Adrian, as we put together the details of this network, you've looked at the 400 count on the laptops, but you do have the alternative of desktops for less money per unit. This will allow you to add on another server. Why don't I put figures in for both, but for your time frame and load, how do you feel about going with the desktop and extra server option? That adds only $250 and gives you another server. What are your thoughts about that?"

> **TALK TIP**
> A huge element of negotiating is asking for what you want. Any trained negotiator will tell you that. You won't always get exactly what you've asked for, but you *certainly* won't get it if you don't ask.

Finally, create hard copy of the terms of the agreement, even prior to having the lawyers draw up the contract. Then, create a pdf file of your document and email it, or even offer a courier or special pickup. Make the follow-up *your* job, not the customer's. Sometimes—more often than we'd like to acknowledge—the customer thinks he or she heard something entirely different on the phone from what appears in the written proposal or contract. Don't leave that possibility sitting out there.

Get the paperwork to the customer the day of the phone agreement if at all possible and check to confirm these are indeed the terms they think they agreed to. Customers often forget exactly what was said. If you have to make changes, you might be in a negotiation again, or there could just have been a lack of understanding. Whichever the case, send the revised version (revised and emailed while you are on the phone with the customer) and gain agreement that the terms and implementation details are the same that the customer agreed to.

NEGOTIATE BY PERSONALITY

Each customer personality type approaches the negotiation stage in a different way, as you'll see in the following descriptions.

The Precise Customer. The **Precise Customer** is motivated by details, details, and more details! The **P** likes to have a recognizable structure in the negotiation, with everything buttoned up. He or she will be put off by any last-minute surprises. Remember also that the **P** will want everything in writing!

> **Quick Notes: Negotiating with the Precise Customer**
>
> - Goal: order; structure.
> - Negotiation approach: ignores relationships; is rigid.
> - Style: detached; nitpicky on details.
> - Weakness: inflexible; predictable.
> - Requires from you: systematic, organized approach; proof (such as white papers, articles, and third-party documentation).

The Energized Customer. The **Energized Customer** is motivated by impulse and the desire to move on. If **E**s feel they have influenced you to change your mind or concede, they have succeeded in the negotiation.

> **Quick Notes: Negotiating with the Energized Customer**
>
> - Goal: to influence you.
> - Negotiation approach: high intensity; may be loud and sound emphatic and energetic.
> - Style: excitable; wants others to be at the same excitement level.
> - Weakness: ignores others; may not listen.
> - Requires from you: maintain enthusiasm; celebrate the decision.

The Assured Customer. The **Assured Customer** is motivated by the desire to reach *one goal* in the outcome. The **A** must reach that goal or feel like he or she has lost. Avoid the win/win approach, because if you "win" at all, this customer has "lost".

> **Quick Notes: Negotiating with the Assured Customer**
> - Goal: victory.
> - Negotiation approach: threatens, demands.
> - Style: hard; perhaps even issues ultimatums.
> - Weakness: digs in and thus may sidestep concessions.
> - Requires from you: position or posture that you are equal.

The Kind Customer. The **Kind Customer** is motivated by the desire to ensure that everyone is happy with the outcome. The **K** takes a long time to make a decision and is cautious about the effects on everyone involved.

> **Quick Notes: Negotiating with the Kind Customer**
> - Goal: agreement and positive effect all around.
> - Negotiation approach: develops relationship.
> - Style: soft; will accept losses if justified.
> - Weakness: easily swayed, but cannot be bullied.
> - Requires from you: agreement and reminder that the decision is good.

Seal the Close

To close the deal, no matter which personality type you are dealing with, say something immediately after the customer says "yes," confirming that you heard a commitment from him or her. This is a very important part of managing the continuation of the sale (oh yes, you're not done yet).

Confirm and celebrate the commitment. As you seal, you should celebrate with the customer, by saying effusively:

- "Great!"
- "That's terrific news!"
- "We'll ship this afternoon."
- "Thank you so much!"
- "I know management will be pleased."
- "Wonderful! We can't wait to get started on the project!"

Voice and tone are critical when you seal a close with a statement like one of these. For some reason, although many salespeople get excited internally when they close a sale, some don't let the customer hear it. Show your pleasure verbally right over the phone.

A Greener Way to Do Business

To celebrate a large sale, plant a tree to help filter the earth of its CO_2. If you don't have the time or the space, go to www.arborday.com and make a donation to have a tree planted in honor of closing the big one!

SAY "THANK YOU."

Sealing the close verbally by affirming the customer's decision and showing your appreciation with a sincere "thank you" is important. Failing to do so after securing a sale can give the customer pause. If he or she does not hear your gratitude as well as your enthusiasm, your customer may begin to question the decision almost immediately; this is known as "buyer's remorse."

Then follow up, by fax or paper, with a handwritten thank-you note with the contract attached. Or send a note on a card, personalized for your business. It might say something along the lines of, "I'm delighted to have your business, and I look forward to working with you."

If you send the contract and thank-you note by mail, some sort of small gift might be included as well: a specialty product from your company, a mug, T-shirt, nice pen, or something personalized. Other gifts that might be appropriate include cookies, chocolates with the company name on them, office products, or small samples. Whether you send a gift or not, be sure to send the handwritten note to personalize the thank-you. (*Note*: When selling to many government entities, they may have ethics codes that do not allow receipt of various gifts. Make sure you know what the rules are so as not to offend a customer.)

INFORM YOUR CUSTOMER OF THE NEXT STEPS

Remember to let your customers know that you are acting on their decision and initiating the delivery process. Keeping up the momentum after the decision is crucial to sealing the close. Customers aren't always certain that the sale is important to you if you fail to commit to the critical next steps in the sale.

Here are some examples of what you can say:

- "I'm delighted that you've decided to go with our company. Let's go ahead and prepare for the next step of getting the order over to our shipping department."
- "Now that we are set to go with the process, we can schedule our consultants to get on-site at your facility by the seventeenth. Will that work out?"
- "That's great we'll be working together. Let's plan on our next steps of . . ."

GET STARTED ON THE INITIAL DELIVERY

Get some part of the purchase sent to the customer right away to ensure that the close has progressed. This delivery may include:

- The display rack that goes with the product.
- The operation manuals.
- Promotional literature, brochures, and samples for resellers.
- Several of the products (if you can't send all 500 they have purchased, send three).
- Cases for the equipment installation.

Even if it is just the mats that go under the office chairs or the warranty certificates, whatever you send is delivery on the customer's decision and further seals the deal, making it unlikely that your customer will back out.

The Payoff

The anxiety of both the buyer and salesperson at the close can be virtually eliminated with a solid presentation using your F-B-C format. The close is the natural result of a harmonious, transactional conversation. Salespeople who are tuned in to the personality type and the real needs of customers close the business. They create solid matches and sales that stick long after they have hung up the phone. Long-term sales relationships create profit for your company while they solve problems for your customers. The close is where you get to cash in on your phone-selling strategy.

Let's see how Mandy is coming along with her sale:

MANDY: Sarah, it sounds like you are ready to move forward. When would you like us to ship the order?

The close is going smoothly because Mandy has acknowledged the customer's reply with something positive. Mandy is also following up with the next step in the closing process: securing the order by asking a question about delivery:

MANDY: Sarah, you seem to be leaning toward using our services. When do you want to get started?

Good. Now Mandy and the customer are in a dialogue about setting a date and moving forward. Let's see where Mandy goes from here:

MANDY: Sarah, you said others are involved in the decision. What's the best way to get them all on the phone together for a conference call?

Excellent. Mandy is asking for a follow-up appointment and moving forward in the sale! That works.

CHAPTER 9

Using New Technology in Phone Sales

PHONE SALES CHALLENGE – *Zachary, a relative newcomer to college textbook sales, has a problem: "In working with the professors I have as customers, I often find that their class schedules make them difficult to reach by phone. Not to mention those committee decisions, where all the professors are either teaching, working with students, or off campus. It's impossible to get them all together! I need a way to have quick exchanges with them between classes and to present to the whole committee at once. How can I do that with just a phone?"*

All salespeople use the phone on a regular basis, regardless of what they are selling. Those of you who are doing inside sales are used to "meeting" your customers this way all the time. But very few salespeople, whether phone-selling veterans or those just recently moved inside, fully utilize the wide range of telecommunications and online technology available to them for managing their customer contacts.

Zachary sounds like he needs a crash course in making the most of his communication choices. Let's eavesdrop on some of his other sales communications first, though, to see what needs to be supported or changed.

> *ZACHARY:* You indicated that there are others involved in your textbook decisions. Will you please send me their names and contact information, so I can call them about our book and software options?
>
> *CUSTOMER:* Well, I'm rather busy today with a class deadline and everybody is at different campuses . . .
>
> *ZACHARY:* That's okay. How about if I call you back later in the week and get the information from you then?
>
> *CUSTOMER:* Okay, whatever you want to do.

In the above scenario, Zachary failed to get the names from the customer while they were still on the phone. Instead of losing valuable time and momentum, he should have asked for access to an administrative person or a departmental directory for that information. Then, once he had the contact information he needed, he could have set up a conference call or webinar in order to speak with all the decision makers at the same time. How many times does a sale fall apart due to the amount of time required to "sell" each person individually?

Out of frustration, Zachary decides that he'll try texting the professor to move the decision along. This is what he sent:

> *ZACHARY (texting):* aamof, if u r ready to make a decision today, we can probly get u some extra desk copies. aap, Zachary
>
> *CUSTOMER (texted reply):* Zachary, I don't understand what you're trying to say. We can't be pushed into making an immediate decision on campus today, though, so don't worry about it.

It's pretty apparent what is happening here, and this is why we discourage texting customers. Zachary's use of excessive acronyms and shortcuts, combined with his lack of attention to proper grammar and punctuation, and his pushy approach, did not serve the situation well. However, if the customer prefers that form of communication, there are times when it is appropriate to contact him or her using that tool. In this instance, clearly the customer didn't appreciate Zachary's method of communication and sent an articulate and yet negative reply that pointed up his lack of professionalism. Texting a customer is not the same as texting a friend to meet for a drink.

Zachary finally decided to schedule a webinar so that he could speak with a number of the decision makers at once and use visuals in his presentation. Let's see how his plan worked out.

Zachary went ahead and scheduled the webinar for a few of the decision makers. This is what happened:

ZACHARY (showing pages from one of his company's textbooks): So as you can see from the charts and tables in the Student's Edition, this book is equipped to provide your students with the most up-to-date information available. And as you can see in this next slide. . .

CUSTOMER 1 (interrupting): How much more time is this going to take? I have a class to teach.

CUSTOMER 2: Yeah, now that you mention it, can you just send us the URL and let us look at the slides? That'll be much quicker. I really don't have time for all this.

CUSTOMER 3: I had a couple of questions, but I'm thinking that I need to run, too. Please be sure to email me attachments with the pages from the book that you showed us and I'll see if what I need to know is in them before we make a decision. I can always call you back later.

Webinars can be useful tools, but Zachary has neglected to keep in mind that presentations with visual elements do not necessarily lend themselves to interactivity. He forgot that selling to several people at a time requires a higher level of planning and activity to keep the participants engaged than selling to one person on the phone. When customers are bored, they come up with excuses to leave your call, real or not. Whether Zachary was violating time constraints that were set up in advance or had just lost the interest of his customers, he was no longer engaged in a sales conversation with them. Anyone want to bet on whether that last professor will call Zachary later to ask a question? And how easy do you think it's going to be for him to set up a webinar with this group in the future?

The Pros and Cons of New Technology

Perhaps five years ago you could have gotten away with avoiding new technology in doing business, but today that has become increasingly difficult. Of course there are still both salespeople and customers, who avoid using the newer forms of communication. However, the vast majority of both salespeople and customers are embracing the accessibility of information and people that multifunction phones, PDAs, email, videoconferencing and webcams, and online chats offer. But before you set up a chat or webinar with a customer and begin tweeting with everyone in your contact list, be sure to take some time to develop strategies for using today's tools appropriately.

Let's look at some of the pros and cons of the different forms of communication now available to the telephone salesperson.

MOBILE PHONE CALLS

In some of the upgraded models, your mobile phone can allow you some of the freedom of a laptop. If you are a total mobile phone communicator, consider the elements that follow.

> *Pros:* Mobile phones are portable; they can be used as a call manager; they hold numbers as well as messages; they offer Internet access; they can be used as a camera; they allow conference calling; they can be used to send and receive emails and to access the Web immediately; and they allow contact with customers outside standard daily business channels.

> *Cons:* Signal quality varies and leaves many "holes" in conversations, including frustrating "dead air" upon answering; calls beeping in can be a distraction to both the salesperson and the customer.

MOBILE PHONE TEXTING OR OTHER INSTANT MESSAGING

With so many devices for instant electronic exchanges, text messaging, or "texting," has become a quick way to touch base with someone from a PDA (a BlackBerry or iPhone device for example), or you can send (and receive) instant messages via your computer email system. Texting can serve you well in the right circumstances, but it can hamper your relationship with the customer in others. Keep in mind that texting is considered informal and best used with internal contacts rather than external customers.

> *Pros:* Texting and instant messaging devices offer a quick way to convey and receive information when urgency is important; they encourage interaction from customers who avoid phone calls; they make it easier to send ideas quickly onto a customer's mobile device for a rapid response.

> *Cons:* These devices make it easier to create errors in spelling, grammar, and capitalization, which can be seen as a lack of professionalism; impersonalized broadcasts are resented as spam; many customers will respond only to urgent text messages from either family members or their employees.

WEBINARS

Webinars are the telecommunication version of the sales presentation to a roomful of people—without you at the front of the room.

> *Pros:* Webinars enable you to give a slide and phone presentation to several decision makers at once; customers watching the presentation on the Internet can be directed to websites or award notices about the company's product or service, which is especially helpful when pictures, complex diagrams, or schematics are used to add to the effectiveness of the presentation; instant feedback can be elicited on any given slide and the presentation can be adjusted accordingly in real time.

> **TALK TIP**
>
> When running a webinar, it's especially important to avoid having customers drift by keeping participants involved in the call to ensure that you are getting through. Asking questions is one good way to do this. "So, how would this affect your business?" "Can someone offer an example of how this happens?" Addressing the participants by name as you talk is another. "Bill, I believe you said these figures came from your department, right?" "Cassandra, these applications would be more for your people."

Cons: The "dizz-out" factor is pretty high for the same reason as in live slide presentations: The attention of your attendees can drift because of overkill in the number of slides. Slide presentations are poor substitutes for emailed information that can be read at a customer's convenience (or not!) or for good (face-to-face or phone) presentations by capable speakers. Phone webinars do not allow the salesperson to determine when customers have left the call.

> **A Greener Way to Do Business**
>
> Delivering group presentations using a Web-enabled program is as green as it gets. You *and* the customers can sit at your respective desks and get a great deal accomplished using just a little electricity—reducing everyone's carbon footprint.

CONFERENCE CALLS

Multiply your sales calls times ten, add some creative management of the participation of those on the call, and you have the potential for a quick decision—but strategy is crucial.

Pros: Conference calls are a great method for using the phone to compound sales efforts and prevent repetition; when handled effectively they can significantly shorten the selling cycle by engaging all decision makers at once; crafted skillfully, with appropriate preparation and follow-up, they can be a one-shot-solution when it comes to closing business over the phone.

Cons: Finding convenient times for all to phone-meet can be a challenge; the salesperson has to work harder at keeping the meeting on track and keeping everyone engaged; sometimes a pack mentality can set in, causing customers to influence each other in the wrong direction.

EMAIL

All you former face-to-face salespeople and anyone who resists picking up the phone for customer selling for any reason, pay special attention here.

Pros: Email allows the salesperson to send out information whenever it is convenient and allows customers to pick up messages when it is convenient for them; more information can be included in an email than in a text message, which is especially important when communicating numerical or complex data; it can allow the salesperson to open a conversation with a customer in a different time zone or a customer who avoids the phone.

Cons: It is very easy to delete an email if the return address is unknown or the subject line is uninteresting; the email can be viewed as spam to an unknowing customer (or to the mail server he or she is using) and ignored accordingly; rarely will business ever be concluded via email, so it should be used to set up a phone conversation or schedule other follow-ups, rather than as an end in itself.

VIDEOCONFERENCING OR WEB CONFERENCING

Some companies have their own videoconferencing setups, while others rent such facilities for important multisite meetings. Both are becoming more popular as travel costs are being reined in and as customer bases become more international.

> *Pros:* Videoconferencing or web conferencing lets the sales person see customers' faces and read body language during the call. Also, video- and web conferencing can be a good basis for follow-up phone business, and perhaps even a close soon after.

> *Cons:* Technology glitches can include a delay in voice and lip movement, shadow-movement, no sound, no picture, or loss of both in the middle of the video meeting. Few people who have experience with video- or web conferencing are lucky enough to avoid suffering through one or many of those glitches, despite the fact that the technology is improving all the time.

ONLINE CHAT

Many of you have probably used online chats for tech support when you have contacted customer service. Now, think of the potential of real-time chats for sales support.

> *Pros:* Chats can be a good way to deal with customers who are far away or who have a specific informational need; messages can be two way, as with instant messaging; new product chats can be set up for multiple customers in real time.

> *Cons:* If the conversation is set up in a chat room, everything both the salesperson and the customer says can be seen by all, which can become chaotic; lag time between the time it takes to key in a question or response and its appearance on the screen can be awkward; if everyone is chatting at the same time, they can seem unresponsive by not answering each message right away. You'll want to concentrate your sales call either by engaging a customer more one-on-one, or with a like-minded group setting, as in a conference call. Also, sim-

ilar to texting, many people abbreviate during chats, and the lack of professionalism doesn't usually lend itself to sales.

Guidelines for the Strategic Use of New Technology

This is the point in the chapter where we have to discuss customers' willingness to engage in one channel of communication or another. And in the same way, it's time to take a hard look at your own preferences. Some businesspeople prefer telephone conversations, while others prefer communications by email, texting, or chats. Their preferences can be driven by any number of reasons, from the need to organize their thoughts by touching keys and looking at ideas as they appear on a screen, to a general aversion to speaking with strangers.

Some clients enjoy seeing supporting documents or drawings to accompany what you, the salesperson, are saying on the phone. They simply process better with visual as well as audio input. Other clients feel more comfortable when they are able to bounce ideas off a group or think out loud by listening and exchanging with colleagues. Pay attention to your own comfort zone as well as your clients'. Use the phone because it works. Support your phone sales with other methods; follow up with electronic or hard copy contracts, agreements, terms of sale, samples, or demos.

Given the varied preferences of your customers, it's important that you not fall into a pattern of making sales contacts using only your own personally preferred style of communication. Many sales situations today have multiple elements and communication media involved, including the phone (both single call and conference calls), email, video exchanges, and web presentations using the phone at the same time. By fully utilizing the strategic advantages of each medium, you can improve your close rate dramatically.

MOBILE PHONE BOUNDARIES

More and more customers are leaving their mobile phone numbers on outgoing voice mail as well as on their business cards. When it

comes to mobile phones, there is definitely a right and a wrong way
to approach them. Just because customers leave their mobile number
on voice mail does not mean that *you* necessarily have permission
to call. Most of your customers are leaving their mobile number on
voice mail so that *their* customers and coworkers can get in touch
with them. That is not an invitation for the rest of us to call those
closely held numbers.

On their voice mail messages, customers don't say, "Here is my
mobile number, but if you are selling, don't call." Keep in mind that
most people who depend on their mobile phones answer them wher-
ever and whenever—often at inappropriate times—and this is not necessarily in your best interest. You want to be able to speak with your
customer when you have their undivided attention and interest.

> **TALK TIP**
> Think of calling your customers' mobile phones this way: If you
> do not already have a relationship with the customer, then you're
> spamming their mobile line.

For general guidelines, it is okay to call customers on their mobile
phone *only if*:

- You have a relationship with the customer and you haven't
  reached him or her after at least three tries on the work line.
- You have left multiple messages (at least five over a period of
  time) and the customer has not returned your call.
- Your customer has invited you to call his or her mobile phone
  and has made it clear that this is the preferred method of getting in touch.

However, if you have determined that it is strategically appropriate to call a customer's mobile phone, remember that you will be interrupting something that he or she is doing—whether it's attending
a meeting, cheering at their child's ball game, leaving the doctor's office, etc.—and that he or she will most certainly not be anticipating

your call. You are inserting yourself into the customer's work or personal life, and for this reason, unless you have a well-prepared opening line, you are more than likely going to be shut down by that customer.

For more detailed guidance, here are a couple of specific situations:

If you have a prior relationship with the customer, when you reach them say, "Sophie, you know I don't like to call you on your cell phone, but I really need to talk with you about the order. Do you have just a moment?" Be sure to wait for the customer's answer on this or you will have lost the good impression you may have made. *If you ask first*, the customer will likely either have a conversation with you then and there or will schedule one with you. With such respectful treatment, she may even apologize for not having returned your previous calls.

If you have no prior relationship with the customer, then you might open your call with, "Hello Mr. Jones, this is (your name). I know you've been very busy, and I needed to get in touch with you about your advertising this year." After your opener, don't ask your customer if he has time to talk. See how it goes. Mr. Jones may choose to speak with you, or reschedule, or just reject your call outright. Keep in mind that before using his mobile phone number you must have made a number of good-faith efforts to reach him through his work line. He will be aware of this, too, since you have already left multiple voice mail messages.

Finally, resist the urge to leave messages on customers' mobile phones unless you have a good relationship with them. Otherwise, you're at risk of alienating them by sounding like a potential stalker. It's generally best to take a conservative approach toward the use of mobile phones, because the likelihood of success is far greater on a landline than it is on wireless service.

PHONE TEXTING

Although texting is a huge social networking phenomenon, the protocols for its use in business are not yet solid. The upside of this is that you can lay some of the groundwork for texting as a business communication option. One of the downsides is the care required to keep business texting and social texting styles separate.

Here are some guidelines:

Keep your text messages short. You are often texting while on the run, and your customer is likely to be reading them under the same circumstances. Text messages are not emails. They must be short and simple, yet able to get across possibly complex ideas. You can elaborate in a later phone call, but urgency may require an instant message—a very brief message. You may want to practice composing messages of 160 characters or fewer.

Avoid letting customers interpret what you are saying. Ambiguity may be seductive and mysterious in social texting, but there is no place for imprecise language in business selling. You might want to try out some of your communications on others to be sure they aren't likely to be misinterpreted. If nothing else, read a text message aloud to yourself before sending it.

Skip the emoticons. Cute textual portraits of your moods or facial expressions—like smiley faces—are for friends and dates, not business associates.

Be careful of the use of italics or fancy fonts. Sometimes services are not compatible, so the formatting you so carefully placed in a text message might not even show up. If you can't get your point across without specialized visual effects, then texting might not be the best medium to be using.

Establish the relationship and reason for the texting strategy before you ever text a customer. If the customer doesn't remember who you are, anything you say will look like spam. You and your customer will need to agree on the use of text messages, and the best way to do this is to tie it to a specific communication need—for both you and the customer. You know, ask: "Shall I send you a text message when I get the figures you asked for, or would you prefer that I leave a message on your office phone?"

FAXING

In the spirit of remaining green, we caution you about the overuse of faxes. The advantages of fax communications, however, are that you may have better control over the appearance of your logo, your formatting, and your typeface. In addition, many people can send and receive faxes from their computers, so you can get signed contracts back in real time with your sales call. Here are some guidelines to follow when you consider faxing:

- Consider a fax instead of an email attachment when a customer's company firewall or antivirus security system might kick out an attachment. Faxes aren't subjected to the same screening.
- Faxes that are being used for prospecting should have detailed delivery information on them—including name, department, and subject—so that they aren't trashed at the fax receiving area.
- Faxes that are properly addressed will sometimes be hand-delivered to your hard-to-reach customer by an obliging colleague—instead of languishing at the fax station.

EMAILING

An email cannot replace a sales presentation as your primary selling tool, but since most businesspeople use email, you can use it effectively as both a contact and a follow-up strategy.

Here are some basic guidelines for using email:

Style: Remember that an email is a written communication, and as such you should observe the conventions of memos and letters that would be sent out in your name. You can tell a lot about a person's education level, professionalism, attention to detail, organization, intelligence, and motivation in an email, and guess what—so can your customer! Sarcasm, exaggeration, and attempts at "dry" humor can be all too easily misinterpreted. And if there is something to misinterpret, the email can be printed out, saved, and shared. Customers will tend to remember your poor communication when a print record is available.

Grammar, punctuation, etc.: A particularly glaring demonstration of your professionalism (or lack of it) is your precision with grammar, punctuation, capitalization, spelling, and language usage. An email is still business communication and should not be confused with casual, social instant messaging that includes abbreviations and the stylized lack of rules that go with it. If you have any difficulties with Standard English written communication (and I'm sure you know if you do), then consider purchasing a business communication handbook or taking a short course to polish your skills in this area. Many are available online.

Use of "you" rather than "I" or "we": Also, remember to use "you" more than "I" or "we." In written communication, we tend to state what *we* want, rather than show the customer what he or she can have with our product or service.

Attachments: When sending attachments, be sure to number and title them. In this way, customers will know what and how many attachments they should have received, in case one gets lost. In addition, don't forget to include the attachments when you send the email. Keep in mind, however, that the security level setting on your customer's network might delete your attachments—which is another good reason to mention them in your cover note.

> **TALK TIP**
>
> A word about editing your emails must go here. You cannot afford to send emails to the wrong person or to send any out with errors. One way to prevent this is to leave off the recipient's email address until *after* you have finished and reread the entire email. Once you have written your email, spell-check it, and then edit for errors in information as well as grammar, punctuation, etc., first. This way, if you have an itchy trigger finger, you won't send out something that isn't professional, saving you potential embarrassment and possibly even rejection.

With the 100 or so emails your customers receive daily, they are likely to expect a certain number of solicitations. Because of this, all subject lines are scrutinized and screened.

Here are some guidelines for creating a good subject line:

Referral: Use a referral person's name in the subject line. Let's say that Frank Franklin has given you a lead to contact Margaret Subbhash. If you send Margaret a direct email about your product or service, she most likely will not open it. If, however, your subject line is, "Frank Franklin," someone she knows, she will be more likely to read your email.

Follow-up: Be simple and direct. A subject line that reads "Following Up" is short and to the point.

Inbound request from customer: Again, simplicity and directness are best. "Your request for proposal" or "Your request for (your) services."

Cold call: You don't want your cold calls to sound too salesy from the beginning. Don't put "Save Money," or "Reduce Wasted Time," or "Don't miss out" in your subject line. These are overdone and sound cheesy (what's in *your* spam folder?). Instead, address a specific or differentiating need or benefit of your product in the subject line: "CPAs Get Certification."

The greeting in your email is important as well. Here are some guidelines:

Options: There are many quality greetings that you can use, including: "Good morning" (regardless of time of day), or "Hello," or "Greetings." "Thank you for . . ." is always welcome as well.

Purpose: A good greeting is a terrific way to gently warm up your customer.

Length: Keep the greeting short and polite.

The body of an email is where you get your message across. Here are some guidelines:

Hook: A hook in the case of a referral might be: "Frank Franklin suggested that I contact you about your interest in organic pet food for your store." If it is not a referral, you might use: "In visiting your store recently I noticed that you do not carry any lines of organic pet food." Or, "You may be aware that with consumers' increased interest in natural products, organic pet food . . ."

Paragraph following the hook: In the paragraph after the hook you might want to set an appointment. For example, "You're probably aware of the emphasis on better nutrition for pets and the increased margins these products can bring you. When is the best time to briefly discuss your pet foods?"

For a cold call first contact, use the following approach: Salutation, greeting, then follow with a strong need or benefit, "Pet Owners are spending 35 percent more on organic pet foods today than ten years ago. This means there are ways to add to your margin with new product offerings that maximize sales. Email me back with your interest in a few free samples, so you can share these with your customers."

Always close cold call emails with "Thank you for the courtesy of your reply." Just this added courtesy line will often elicit a response from customers.

For a follow-up on a prior contact, use this approach: Salutation, greeting (in this case the greeting would be a "thank you"), and then, "Thank you for sharing with me your store's pet food growth plan. In your market area it appears you have a sizable demand for organic pet food products. As promised, we will be sending you a carton of samples for your consideration. When is the best time next week to follow up with you on this?"

For a warm call with an existing customer, try this approach: Salutation, then, "Thank you for carrying our products in your stores. Your customers probably appreciate the product quality and the availability of organic foods.

"You may want to take advantage of our spring supersale. For every two pallets of product purchased, you will receive one pallet at half price. I will be calling you in the next two days to check with you for an order.

"Again, thank you for your continued business and we look forward to serving your needs as you increase margins."

A signature line brings your email to a close. Here are some guidelines:

Set up a default signature line: This should include your name, title, company, phone number, email address, and website URL. You can also include a sales line, "Visit our website for 100% organic pet foods."

A differentiation line might be effective as well: A differentiator—"Register for our weekly sales tips newsletter," or "Earn an additional case with every purchase"—is one of your competitive advantages. This type of addition must be legal and okayed by your company.

Less is more: Your words are not all golden, and your customer's attention span is very short. Make sure your message is as succinct as you can make it.

Finally, never send a first draft—always *edit*. Can't say this often enough.

VIDEOCONFERENCING

Videoconferencing can certainly enhance communication, but as noted earlier there are many pitfalls for you to be on the alert for. Here are some guidelines for using videoconferencing in your business:

Test, test, test: If at all possible, draft a technician at the other end of the videoconference to run through about five minutes of exchanges. Pay attention to volume, mike location, and "ghost movement" issues. Particularly note delay time. The more aware you are of the limitations of the situation, the better you can guide the others for the best experience. For example, you might suggest that pairs or threes cluster around microphones throughout the room, or if they are using a centered table mike, ask speakers to move to the mike area when they wish to speak.

Clothing: As with any group presentation where you are the focus, be careful what you wear. Wear nothing too casual or too "busy." Sometimes the picture is a bit distorted and a complex pattern in clothing would be very distracting.

Mobile phones: Ask everyone to turn off their mobile phones.

Guideline sheets: It can be helpful to send out a brief videoconference guideline sheet to remind people that they are in camera view and mike range nearly all the time. An embarrassing mannerism might not be visible in a phone conference call, but could be projected to your company's entire French customer group on video!

Slides: Slides can be difficult to see even when the audience is in the room, but a projected slide sent by a videocam is hazy at best. Better to find a way to have Web access for participants to see slides on their own laptops. You can control the conference presentation somewhat by better positioning the slides presented—order, rate of display, etc.

WEBINARS AND CONFERENCE CALLS

Webinars and conference calls are grouped together because they have many of the same challenges. First, however, let's briefly look at the unique opportunity with webinars. Webinars have in many instances replaced the sales presentation made in person to a roomful of people. Remember, though, webinars are still presentations—although you are not in the room with your audience, and so you will need to engage listeners—and for that reason you will need to follow some rules to make them successful.

This is not the place for a discussion of the effective construction of slides to which you will direct participants while you share a conference call with the attendees. As a general rule, though, slides should be a backbone, not a script on the screen. Use visuals and diagrams to illustrate processes or any type of flow instead of a numbered list of steps. Use art to emphasize the points being made in the bullets. Finally, keep the number of slides to a minimum; make sure they are interesting, preferably exciting; limit yourself to offers of proof, testing data, testimonials, awards, and similar elements that have visual impact.

Now, since your webinar and/or teleconference can allow your customers to drift off into their own enterprises and not pay attention, here are the ways to keep everyone involved. You must E-N-G-A-G-E. Here are some guidelines:

E—*EXCITE participants with your enthusiasm and motivating style.* This is a presentation, not a regular call, so listeners will draw their level of involvement from you. Put energy into your tone, your pronunciation, and your inflection. Vary the pace at which you speak, however, or you can become monotonous—you know, like those commercials where the guy yells at you to buy products. Also, if you stand up and walk around while you are on the call, you will come across stronger in your presentation. Remember to smile— you'll sound better—and use humor occasionally.

N—*NURTURE* participation by good planning. Send out an agenda with pertinent items to be discussed. Use your advance research to ensure that you have chosen just the right products or benefits or solutions for this group. You want to hit hot buttons often, not just do a feature fling and hope something sticks. In addition, talk with some of the participants in advance and ask them to share stories or statistics that would interest the others. Prepare yourself with a list of all participants so that you can keep track of who is speaking and who may be holding back for some reason.

G—*GUIDE* the meeting. This is a meeting, you see, a meeting that you have called, so it is up to you to keep it going and on track. Whether you have twelve decision makers from one company on one deal or a hundred participants from a hundred different companies to announce a new product, you can still keep everyone involved with good questioning techniques. Don't be afraid to shift gears to a new slide or topic if interest is waning. Check-ins are good for this, and you can use names: "Martin, how does this approach fit in with the system your team is looking at?"

Now, this part is a bit tricky. You may get "dead air" after you question Martin, because he may be managing his eBay account while you are making critical points. If this happens, *never* embarrass the participant by calling him out. Instead, say, "You know, Martin, this might be a good time to get a reaction from everyone. Do you mind if I open the question to everyone?" Martin is off the hook, but likely paying attention now—as are the others who might be called on.

A—*ADVANCE* the sale. You knew we were going to say that, didn't you? Build relationships during the webinar or conference call. You have customers on the phone, so by using questioning and check-ins you should be building not only rapport but buy-in. And the good thing is that a group dynamic can help you start the momentum toward the close. You've been to auctions, haven't you? That's what occurs with auction bidding. Several positive responses to check-ins can help to influence others when they hear agreement in voices other than yours.

G—*GAIN* commitments and keep track of them. Make notes of the elements of your presentation that have gotten positive reactions from the participants. Also note who hasn't spoken too much or at all. (Your agenda should have a list of all who are watching the presentation, both for your benefit and for those who are there.) Be sure to pull those people into the conversation so that you aren't blindsided by an off-the-wall question or concern. It's better to draw them in than to wait for a zinger. Plus, the affirmation provided by the attention you pay in asking for their opinion or input can strengthen the support for your close.

E—*END* on a positive note. Be certain to watch the time and begin to close five minutes before sign-off. You might be finalizing a contract in the call, which would be an ideal close opportunity, or you may just be gaining the foothold you need to get to the next step. Either way, you want to make sure that all questions from customers have been answered and that *you* are the final speaker.

You will end with a summary of the high points, your final motivating point, and a "thank you" for participants by name (if it's a small group). If the group is large or you don't know them all, thank them as a group, then say, "Best wishes in your business today" (or something similar). Today, very few people wish someone well without a specific reason. You might stand out for sending an affirmation their way.

The Payoff

There are so many ways to approach customers these days, but you have to remember what your goal is with every contact—to advance the sale. Some customers will prefer a conference call to an individual call, especially where there are multiple decision makers. You will be able to text some customers for the final details of a negotiation or a confirmation of a price break. Stay on the alert, though, for occasions where you begin to fall into one type of communication technology/ medium for all contacts. The phone should be the beginning, the middle, and the end. The others should be support steps along the way.

Now it's time to check in on Zachary:

ZACHARY: You indicated that there are others involved in the textbook decisions. Can I quickly get their names, and then we can work on setting up a convenient webinar with the team?

CUSTOMER: Sure. There's Yancy Johnson, Sarah Quinn, and Ronaldo Rodriguez.

ZACHARY: Great. I'll get in touch with them right away and see about setting up an Outlook Calendar invitation. Will that be okay with you?

CUSTOMER: Yes. That'll be fine. I look forward to the conference call and learning more about the options.

Zachary has learned, apparently, that customers will help you do your job if you make it easy for them. He's also learned to use new technology to create greater efficiency where a group decision is needed.

ZACHARY (texting): Hello. You asked me to send you the final contract amount for the department, which is $14,567. Would you like us to send over the agreement this afternoon for approval? Thank you. Zachary

CUSTOMER (texting): Sounds good. Yes, go ahead and send the contract over and we'll start the paperwork with the dean.

Much better! He's using texting to finalize a deal and he doesn't come across as a high schooler texting friends during lunch.

CHAPTER 10

Selling to Customers from Other Cultures

PHONE SALES CHALLENGE *– Brenda, an experienced saleswoman, has recently moved into international passenger truck and van sales, and is facing this problem: "I know some French and some Spanish, but it's not just the language thing. It's hard enough figuring out how some of these Europeans think, let alone how to strategize the accounts in India I've just been given, and my customers there speak English!"*

Just as we look at selling to different personality types, when we look at selling to customers in other cultures we must first consider our own culture, because that is the basis of our interpretation of others. Assertive and submissive behavior, as well as agreement and disagreement speaking patterns, are very different among the world's cultures. Silence during the conversation is a pointed example. Americans are often uncomfortable with it and rush to speak, thinking that silence on the other end of the phone means inattention or hesitation. Depending on who the salesperson is speaking with, silence could signal serious consideration of the options presented. Breaking the silence—a typically American phone behavior—might derail what was working into a close. With so many variables in cultural styles, smart phone salespeople in the United States need to learn to recognize differences in stalling, negotiating, or closing signals from their non-American customers.

It might be helpful for you to know how Americans are perceived by some people in other countries:

We're all "cowboys." People in many countries find the "Old West" element of American society endearing, but dislike the galloping-in-with-guns-blazing approach sometimes used in doing business. Americans, and particularly businesspeople, are often seen as pushy, in a hurry, and at times, disrespectful.

Americans care most about money, not relationships. Often we get right down to business without any social niceties or discussion of factors that might affect the person we're speaking with, whether it's a family situation, something in the news, or even the weather.

Americans are "new" and crass. Compared to those from civilizations that are thousands of years old, we're an infant culture and are sometimes viewed as unappreciative of important matters of tradition and protocol.

Ouch! Anyone who has traveled can attest to these perceptions. A compliment by an American about how quaint a pub in England is may prompt the comment, "Well, you can't buy it" from one of the locals. Or an effusive handshake offered to someone from Japan or Korea may be met with an almost painful-looking recoil. So even though you won't be in the pub or shaking hands as you do business over the phone, observing the protocols of other cultures can be useful in developing relationships and securing business.

As you can see from the examples that follow, you may not be the only one who makes mistakes when calling on customers living in or from another country.

> **RYLIE (office furniture saleswoman, calling on a German customer):** Hans,
> you will really, really *love* the way our beautiful mobile furniture fits into
> your work space. It is so flexible, so warm, so friendly—it'll be great!
> The chairs will feel like you are sitting in butter.

Rylie is giving a nearly poetic, sensual description to a customer
from a culture that emphasizes engineering excellence. (Ever drive a
BMW?) As a result, she may be perceived as either lacking in relevant
knowledge or as trying to cover up for a poorly engineered product.
Either way, she has missed the focus that is most important to the
customer—whether it's the technical or engineering detail—and she
has likely lost a sale.

> **ELENA (trade show business entertainment, selling to a Japanese cus-**
> **tomer):** Takumi, I know we haven't spent a lot of time together, but it's
> really great that you want to do business with our firm. After all, every-
> one wants to book our talent for their trade show booths, and as you
> know, we're the most experienced in the market, so you'll really like
> what we offer. I'm sure of that.

> **CUSTOMER:** Yes, thank you for bringing that to our attention.

Oh, Elena, no! Relationship is an important element in doing
business not only with Japanese businesspeople, but with those in the
other Pacific Rim countries as well. It sounds like Elena has not had
time to establish a solid relationship. Bandwagon appeals and boast-
ing don't fly when doing business with individuals in the Pacific Rim.
(In fact, using the words "most" or "best" are frowned upon as self-
aggrandizing.) As for the "yes" she received, it was merely a polite affirmation that she was heard, not that her message was appreciated
or received positively. Sorry, Elena, no sale today.

> **MARCUS (picture frame salesman, selling to a Venezuelan customer):**
> *Buenos días,* Alegría. How's your soccer team doing? Kickin' it? Ha
> Ha. Let's get right to it. You said you really need to get your boss in-
> volved, but if you go ahead and make a decision on the picture frame
> shipment today, we can offer you an additional 10 percent discount.
> Whaddaya say?

Marcus, how could you? First, the most popular sport in Venezuela is baseball, not soccer. Second, leadership and team stability are viewed as very important, so trying to cut the boss out of the negotiation will almost assuredly nix a deal. Negotiations in most Latin countries take quite a long time, so quickie discount pressure is not likely to be well received. Oh, Marcus, you'd better stick to stateside selling, or read a good book on selling to customers in other cultures!

Paying attention to cultural differences is very much a part of telephone selling, especially with the technology available today that closes geographic distances. With so many electronic communication options, Brenda could just as easily cover a sales territory that includes Belgium, France, Canada, or one of the African nations that have French as one of their official languages. But just because she speaks the language doesn't mean she speaks the culture.

Each culture around the world has its own way of expressing its values and expectations. Earlier in this book you considered different personality types and adapted your phone sales strategy to better communicate with those personalities. Now, whether you are calling on customers outside of your country or you are dealing with a customer who has moved here from elsewhere, you need to focus that same attention on cultural variables as you make your phone calls.

The Importance of Time

One of the many differences among cultures is the way in which they view time. If you've set up a conference call or webinar to begin at 9 A.M. in Germany, you're expected to already be on the call when your customers dial in at 9:00—and trust us, they *will* dial in at 9:00, on the nose. Punctual as a culture, Germans are highly insulted if you are late or if you dawdle in getting to the point. Venezuelans, in many ways very Americanized in their business understanding, will expect you to be on time or early as well. On the other hand, a call to another South American country might begin closer to 9:30 and proceed at a more leisurely pace with at least as much casual conversation as business presenting going on. As for customers in the Pacific Rim, they will often do business over dinner after work, and will expect that you do likewise. Be prepared for phone presentations when it is after 6 P.M. in that part of the world.

> **TALK TIP**
> You can expect businesspeople in countries like the United States, Canada, Germany, and Switzerland, and in Scandinavia to be very much into sequential, step-by-step approaches that observe time constraints strictly. The Japanese do business similarly, though circumstances can justify changes in time schedules. Mediterranean and Latin cultures—including France, Italy, Greece, and Mexico, as well as some Eastern and African cultures—are more likely to view a transaction's time limit to be "as long as it takes," because the business includes concerns with not only the transaction itself, but also the effect on all the people involved in the transaction.

Another factor involving time is the rate at which resolution is reached in business. In China, for example, a country whose culture has existed for several thousand years, your need to close business in one or two phone calls might be seen as laughable. Old cultures view time as a bit less important; time and business are about the long run. Consequently, you should expect to give your phone presentation many times, as you will likely deal with several levels of decision makers. The harmony of the decision with both the past and the future is viewed as more important than a quick resolution.

The Role of the Relationship

The role of the relationship in the business process varies among cultures as well. To Americans, this might be best explained in terms of getting to the point versus getting to the person. Getting to the point focuses on written contracts and directly addressing conflicting views or problems. But getting to the person directs attention to formalities of respect and cultivating a trusting connection with the customer—often over time. Hierarchy also plays into the selling situation. In India, for example, you may establish a great relationship with an employee, but decisions are typically made only from the top. Thus, making the sale may involve working through various levels to achieve an introduction to the higher-up, which as you may guess is a longer process than Americans are used to.

> **TALK TIP**
> Getting to the right person in a business deal may involve becoming accepted by the entire group of decision makers. This can necessitate several phone calls, but the process can be sped up by hosting a videoconference. If not possible, posting a picture of yourself during a webinar and asking the other participants to do the same can be useful in establishing a feeling of recognition and camaraderie. And speaking of recognition, you must be aware of the hierarchy at your customers' business—and respect it. Some businesspeople reflect their culture's emphasis on title and position. When you post a picture for your webinar or set up your videoconference, be sure to have the participants' names and titles in plain view.

Another relationship-based cultural variable involved in phone sales is the degree to which "small talk" is involved in the process. Whereas American businesspeople tend to jump right in and ask probing questions or launch directly into discussing product benefits or establishing their company's solid reputation, in Central America and in India polite conversation always takes place before business. And since family is extremely important in both of these cultures, a customer may want to talk about his or her children in leading up to the business conversation. Certainly an inquiry from you about the customer's family would be well received—and might help distinguish you from other, more brusque sales reps.

Many relationship issues, such as the subtleties of eye contact or body language, which vary by culture, can be avoided simply because the phone gives you visual anonymity. However, when a videoconference is scheduled, you would do well to study the nonverbal cues that are predominant in your customer's culture as they relate to respect, acceptance, and interest (we give you a website and a book referral later in this chapter). For example, when conducting a videoconference, consider as part of your planning process what you are wearing and what the camera shows. A loud shirt or a messy desk can be interpreted as disrespectful or "typically American" when viewed by someone from another culture.

Yet another part of the phone selling process is the ability to establish relationships that can moderate the customer's concern with risk, and here, too, cultural differences can be a factor. What you may see as a very low-risk situation according to the numbers, may be viewed as high-risk if the purchase decision conflicts in any way with cultural traditions and formal social rules. For instance, attempting to sell long-term care insurance to a Chinese prospect for her mother would be considered an insult. Chinese people often have extended family living with them, so this sales call most likely would not result in a close. No matter how much relationship-building you do with customers regarding their perception of risk, you will never win them over on the basis of trust alone. You will have to show a compatibility of your product or service with their established cultural values.

A Greener Way to Do Business

Since 2006 the world's major cities have implemented plans to reduce carbon emissions. Companies from international Fortune 100s to small, local businesses are reporting specific and documentable decreases in pollution output. Individuals are driving hybrid cars and installing solar panels on rooftops. Green has become a way that companies can not only do good things for the environment but also do well financially. As a phone salesperson you may be asked about the environmental impact or green practices of the company you represent. Are you ready with good answers to those questions?

Language and Communication Across Cultures

Understanding grows out of common experience. If you know a friend is afraid of spiders, then when you hear a barrage of swear words and a commotion from the garage, you probably aren't alarmed. You can guess that your friend ran across a spider. Your understanding of your common background with your friend made the words, tone, and volume inoffensive. In short, you blew it off as nothing. In a different situation, someone swearing boisterously and throwing things around might either make you angry or scare you.

This is why the context of language is at least as important as the words themselves. You must understand the cultural basis of the communication you are hearing on the phone. And at least as important, your customer must understand the words and phrasing that you use in your sales call as well.

Business communication improves with neutral language—that is, words and sentence structures that are as close to standard as possible. Someone learning English in a foreign country rarely learns casual American English. The person would learn Standard English from a textbook, which would include standard pronunciation, sentence structure, and grammar.

Once you become aware of any casual speech habits that you have, including dropped words or letters at the ends of words, you can begin to adjust your style for phone conversations with nonnative speakers. A refresher in Standard English grammar and pronunciation might be in order. Remember that no one actually speaks Standard English, but the closer you can come to a structured communication style with your customers, the better your rapport will be. Of course this is hard work! But isn't a potential hundred thousand or million dollar account worth it?

Being able to communicate effectively with people from other cultures involves knowing what *not* to do as well as knowing what to do. For instance, when selling to customers from other cultures, you want to be careful not to use too many idiomatic expressions and "typically American" expressions, which can be confusing. For example, "Whatcha' say we pick up some carryout?" or sports analogies such as "You'll hit a home run on this one" are often confusing to people who are trying to understand your words as they would be translated literally. A reference to American baseball expressions would be ludicrous when used with someone from a country where baseball is not played.

It's also wise to play it safe by avoiding any humor, much of which may be perceived as inappropriate, derogatory, or simply misplaced in a business call. A case in point: joking about or poking fun at the Queen is common among the British, but is considered grossly inappropriate by any outsiders.

In addition, it pays to be wary of communicating too casually. Keep in mind that using terms such as "you guys," when referring to a group, can be considered offensive.

> **TALK TIP**
>
> Before you run out and buy a language-learning CD for a call to a specific country, be certain that you know the language of the decision makers. In Brazil you'll find a large German population as well as a sizable Japanese community inside a Portuguese-speaking country! Belgium and Switzerland both recognize several languages, and the Spanish in Spain varies significantly from the Spanish spoken in Guatemala or Mexico. And while many of your customers in other countries will appreciate your attempts at greetings or communication in their language, they might actually prefer to conduct business in English. Just remember to slow down a bit if you are a fast talker, because the customer may have to translate in his or her head as you speak.

But we really need to look beyond mere dos and don'ts of phone conversations across cultures, because communication of intent is what the salesperson banks on. For example, are you focusing on the objections rather than the points of agreement? Are you offended by the Russian customer who argues with you loudly or the French customer who may even become verbally abusive when it comes to stating his or her goals? When you learn that the Russian is arguing to show respect to your viewpoint (he wouldn't be arguing if he didn't see some merit in what you are saying), does that change your perception of the sell-ability of that customer? And though perhaps that French customer is yelling, if you listen closely you may find that she is being quite clear about what she needs to be able to give you a "yes."

Culture and Personality

Now, before you begin to wring your hands over the scope of the challenge of dealing with customers who come from other cultures, go back to the discussion of the four personality types in Chapter 3. From the information in this chapter you will note some similarities of cultural operating styles and personality styles. Germans, for instance, might be seen to fit many of the characteristics of the **Assured** personality type. Central American customers, on the other hand, may be more along the style of the **Kind** personality. Customers from countries in the Middle East are likely to behave like the **Precise** personality type in their strict adherence to rules and procedures. As for Americans, they are most often perceived by much of the rest of the world as fitting the mold of the **Energized** personality perfectly.

As you begin working with customers from different cultures—both those living abroad and those who have settled in the United States—take the time to relate their cultural style to a specific personality type. Naturally you will want to familiarize yourself with more elements of the culture than just enough for a personality match. Also, not every element of a sales exchange is cultural; different personalities exist in all cultures. For this reason the personality work that you do can transcend perceived cultural differences.

Dealing with Cultural Differences

As you might have guessed, there are far too many cultural differences and concerns to cover in a single chapter. The best way to ensure successful phone sales business deals is to heed the following pieces of advice:

- If selling to a customer with whom you are unfamiliar, ask around before calling him or her, or conduct some online research to learn where he or she is from, before making that first call.
- Prior to dealing with a customer from another culture, regardless of whether you have been to their country or know someone from there, research the culture extensively *before* picking up the phone or setting up a webinar or web conference.
- Take cues from the customer's voice mail and writing. You may hear a familiar accent in the outbound voice mail or see a particular writing pattern in an email. These may help you determine how to communicate with that customer, for instance, whether to address him or her more formally by using a surname (Ms. Hyashi) or to use their first name only (Rodrigo) when leaving a message on their answering machine or communicating via email.

Although the authors have both used Morrison and Conaway's comprehensive book, *Kiss, Bow or Shake Hands*, there are numerous other guides available that can also help you to prepare for selling to customers from other cultures. In addition, you may find the following website useful as you add to your education in international phone sales: http://www.beyondintractability.org/essay/culture_negotiation. This site offers many guidelines for expected behaviors and motivations for cultures throughout the world and is set up for easy access to specific information. It also has an extensive listing of further references.

However, for a quick overview to help you in doing business with certain cultures, see Table 10-1.

The Payoff

The worldwide recession beginning in 2008 proved pointedly that we are all participants in a world economy. But while we are inter-

Table 10-1　Customers Around the World

	Forms of Address	Negotiation Style	Communication Style	Avoid This
CANADIANS	First name if you know the person. More formal until invited.	Disagree tactfully. Like to have facts and documentation.	Pragmatic. Minimal small talk. Community-oriented.	Asking personal questions. Making exaggerated claims.
MEXICANS	Informal but hierarchical in approach.	Utilize "machismo" in negotiations. Run late, and deadlines are fluid. Hagglers.	Promote rank as important. Pleasantries and conversation before business.	Pushing for a deadline. Disregarding their hierarchy in the organization.
GERMANS	Formal. Use surnames. Titles and academic backgrounds important.	Rigid protocol. Formal. Very decisive. Blunt.	Plan far in advance and are inflexible about changing plans.	Showing too much emotion. Making claims without documentation. Mixing personal questions with business.
JAPANESE	Formal with surnames.	Nonconfrontational. Say "yes" to mean "I understand." Negotiate in groups.	Formal and ritualized style. Like personal relationships with exceptional service. Soft-spoken.	Raising voice and getting too loud or emotional. Confrontation. Being late for meetings. Saying "no."
CHINESE	Formal with surnames.	Are shrewd negotiators. Rank is important in negotiating. Are nonconfrontational.	Concerned about rank, decorum. Very punctual. Measured and controlled speaking style.	Using high-pressure tactics. Showing impatience. The word "no." Too much informality or effusiveness.

UK CITIZENS	Formal with titles or surnames.	Like written communication. Are direct but modest.	Reserved emotions. Are sticklers with protocol and formality. Like long-term relationships.	Being late to meetings even with time difference. Showing too much emotion or enthusiasm. Being too casual or personal.
SAUDI ARABIANS	Formal.	Are tough negotiators. Repeat points to gain credibility.	Are relationship builders. Judge by appearances. Are slow decision makers.	Making afternoon appointments. Using high-pressure tactics.
KOREANS	Formal.	Adopt the "less is more" approach. Contracts are loose.	Use relationship as foundation for doing business. Are direct and concise.	Asking closed-ended questions. Talking too much.
VENEZUELANS	Formal and hierarchical.	Decide after meetings. Are slow decision makers.	Need to feel a trust. Are risk-averse.	Making afternoon appointments. Being too loose and informal. Friday afternoon business.
FRENCH	Formal.	Trust those who show proper behavior. Work through secretaries.	Are direct. Ask probing questions. Formal written communication through assistants. Are low-key and logical.	July, August appointments. Being late. Sloppy contracts. Exaggerated claims.

dependent on larger economic levels, salespeople operate at the company- or individual-decision level where the impact of the recession is looked at in different ways. Thus, you need to understand thoroughly the basis for decision making used by the culture of the customer you are selling to. The more you know about the rules and perceptions of the nature of business in each country you deal with, the greater the success you will have.

If you can become comfortable and effective doing business globally, you will be a valuable asset to your company. And that is job security.

So it's time to see how secure the salespeople that we eavesdropped on earlier have become:

> **RYLIE:** Hans, there are two reasons you will want to consider placing our mobile furniture in your office space. First of all, based on your office blueprints, the furniture's streamlined edges will fit perfectly into the geometric design of your space. Second, you mentioned that you are concerned about maintaining the office integrity by creating a consistent look throughout the building. This furniture meets those outlined specifications.

Good job, Rylie! Her approach demonstrates an attention to detail not only in the references to blueprints, specs, and design, but also in the sequential organization of the presentation.

> **ELENA:** Mr. Ono, thank you kindly for taking the time to speak with me about your upcoming trade show. Based on your requirements, it appears that there are a variety of people involved in this decision at your firm. As a next step, what do you think about us scheduling a conference call to discuss what your colleagues are thinking?

Elena has smartened up considerably in the way she deals with her Japanese customer. She has used a formal approach, addressing the customer by his last name. Plus, she has affirmed the need for consensus in the decision-making process and suggested a medium that will include others. Now she has an opportunity to move forward in this sales interaction.

MARCUS: Alegría, hello and best wishes to you and your family. They tell me in the office that your nephew lives in Miami with your brother and plays ball in the minors there. How are they doing?

CUSTOMER: Ah, Marcus, actually my nephew's team has won three in a row. Thank you for asking. And your daughter, is she playing basketball this year?

MARCUS: Yes, she is, and I'm very proud of her. My family is very important to me and I want to always make sure they have a good life, just like you do, Alegría.

CUSTOMER: Of course. My youngest will finish school this year. We are also very proud.

MARCUS: That's excellent. My best wishes go to them all. (Pause) I do remember that you had asked me to call to discuss the framing options in more detail. However, we wouldn't want to rush you into moving too quickly. We're on your time frame. Do you think that we should look into web conferencing with you and your managers so that we can answer your questions and show you some options within our line?

Marcus seems to be learning about the speed of business and the role that cultivating relationships plays in conducting business over the phone with customers from other cultures. Now he is looking forward to better managing his relationships by selling more over the phone to close more business *and* make more money!

PEAK Personality Type Assessment

Who Am I?

Examine the four adjectives in each grouping. Rank the adjective that *best* describes you with a 7, the next closest a 5, the next closest a 3, and the least descriptive adjective with a 1. Use each number only once in each set.

1. ____ (**A**) punctual

   ____ (**E**) enthusiastic

   ____ (**K**) family-oriented

   ____ (**P**) orderly

2. ____ (**A**) adventurous

   ____ (**E**) life of the party

   ____ (**K**) moderate

   ____ (**P**) precise

3. ____ (**A**) stubborn

   ____ (**E**) persuasive

   ____ (**K**) gentle

   ____ (**P**) humble

4. ____ (**A**) competitive

   ____ (**E**) playful

   ____ (**K**) obliging

   ____ (**P**) obedient

5. ____ (**A**) determined

   ____ (**E**) convincing

   ____ (**K**) good-natured

   ____ (**P**) cautious

6. ____ (**A**) assertive

   ____ (**E**) optimistic

   ____ (**K**) lenient

   ____ (**P**) accurate

Add each letter's value by transferring the numbers to the bottom of this form below each letter and totaling. (For example, 16 **P**s, 24 **A**s, and so forth.) Note your highest numbers to determine your natural style.

P	**E**	**A**	**K**
____	____	____	____

SOURCE: © Renee Walkup, SalesPEAK, Inc. All rights reserved, 678 587.9911 www.salespeak.com

Handling Customer Complaints Effectively

Salespeople rarely receive a call from customers thanking them for their help in making their purchase. More often than not, the call we receive after the sale closes is from the customer who has an issue. The reason you receive this call and not Customer Service is that customers align themselves with their salesperson. Because you have developed a trusting relationship with your customers, they often will come to you with their problems, bypassing other company employees who may be officially designated to help them. Now that there's an issue, the customer wants you to fix it. And make it right.

When you receive a customer complaint, it's important that you respect the relationship because it includes your company as well. Many times repeat business is awarded based on how a customer is treated *after* the sale. Since you may be the first line of communication, it is in your best interest to handle that call the best way possible.

Every salesperson knows that if a customer isn't satisfied after the sale, the idea of a "repeat customer" won't exist. Whether your company has a group of Customer Service Reps (CSRs) or not, the reality is that more times than not, the customer will come to you for help, advice, and resolution when a problem arises.

What kinds of complaint patterns can you expect? Let's take a brief look the four personality types to see their behavior when under stress.

Precise Customers do not want to pick up the telephone to call until they have all of their facts written down and prepared in advance. This type of customer knows *when* the delivery took place, *who* was involved, *what* time the purchase arrived, and *what* exactly the issue is. Because the **P** is organized before calling you with the concern, chances are the details are highly accurate. Remember how they are motivated by the facts? This behavior remains the same when the **P** calls with an issue.

Your highly emotional **Energized Customers** will call when they have the time. That could mean sometime between their 12:55 and 1:00 appointment! Es tend to ramble, straying off the issue, and may not bother to have the serial number, time, or correct names in front of them when they call. The typical **E** rattles off the complaint, anticipating resolution within seconds—even though valuable information may be missing from his or her end of the line. Expect some drama from this type of customer.

The **Assured Customer** expects results. And fast! This type of customer immediately launches into a rant about what is needed to correct the problem. The **A** does not want you to make excuses or take the time to research the issue. In other words, he or she does not care about why, how, or who; the **A** only cares about when and how you intend to remedy the problem. The natural personality of the **A** is to raise his or her voice and bark out orders when stressed.

Because **Kind Customers** do not want to jeopardize the good relationship that has been built, and tend to be more passive in their approach, they are similar to Ps when there's an issue. Ks tend to have their information prepared before calling, and are never demanding in their approach. He or she may sound calm, but don't let that gentle voice fool you. There is a problem and you must resolve it in the best way possible. If ignored, the **K** will seek a higher level of influence in your company.

Keep in mind that most customers under stress have mentally shifted to their emotional operating style, which often means that logic has ceased to exist.

Now that you have a clearer understanding of expected personality customer approaches when there's an issue, let's take a look at the seven steps that you can take to resolve complaints with skill and professionalism:

Step 1. Make the right first impression. Answer the telephone with a warm, inviting voice—*always!* Even if you *know* this is an irate customer on the other end of the telephone. Your confident, in-control voice makes it clear that you are ready to help and aren't afraid to speak with your customer. If you have a customer under stress on the other end of the phone, this approach may also immediately calm them down and remind them that you are willing to help.

Step 2. Listen without interrupting. Despite the personality of the customer on the other end of the phone, he or she needs to be listened to. All the way through. The better you are at remaining quiet and hearing out the problem, the more successful you will be at resolving the customer's issue. Remember that your goal is to solve the problem *and* maintain a long-term customer. So be quiet, and listen just as intently as if you were making a sale, and *take notes!*

Step 3. Summarize what you heard. It's important to first make sure you are clear what the issue is, then that the customer understands that you have been listening to what they have been saying, and finally that you consider the problem important and will do what you can to solve it. Be brief when you recap the situation and refer to the careful notes you took while the customer was explaining the problem. Keep your voice *neutral*—not emotional, disgusted, argumentative, or distraught.

Step 4. Investigate if necessary. If the complaint requires some research from your end, either ask the customer if you can call them back or whether they can hold. It's important that you offer the customer a choice: It empowers the customer and reinforces your acknowledgment of the situation. A favorite transitional phrase while working through a customer's problem is, "Let's see what we can do . . ." By saying this you are indicating that you have listened, but are not making any promises at this point in the conversation. If no research is required, go to Step 5.

Step 5. Offer two solutions. Again, customers love to have choices. We all do. If there was a shipping problem and the wrong item was delivered to Tim's loading dock, ask him if he would prefer to return the incorrect shipment or simply keep it at a discounted price. Or, you can ask whether he would rather have the product shipped overnight or two-day air. There are thousands of these combinations from which to chose, depending, of course, on the complaint, your company policies, and other variables. Just resist the urge to say "We'll do *this*," when you can offer the customer a *choice*.

Step 6. Get an agreement from the customer. After you have provided your customer with two choices, ask for an agreement. For example, you may ask, "Do you want us to credit your account or provide you with an additional pallet of material?" Then be quiet and wait for an answer. In this way, your customer will feel empowered to make the decision. After you are told which choice the customer prefers, close off the interaction. You might say, "Tim, we'll have that pallet on the truck in the morning and you'll have it by Wednesday afternoon. Okay?"

Step 7. Close in a positive way. Thank Tim for bringing the issue to your attention and reinforce the fact that you appreciate his business as an important long-term customer. Also, remember to confirm that the solution you came up with did, indeed, solve the problem. While you may not want to ask this question for fear of opening up a new can of worms (you are *not*, after all, your company's customer service department), if the problem has not been resolved to the customer's satisfaction you will certainly hear about it again. Better to be prepared with a follow-up call placed at a time that is convenient for you and not be blindsided by the customer calling you back to continue his or her complaint.

So, if you want more business, (and who doesn't), make sure that you are taking care of your customers by addressing their complaints professionally. And the next time you get on the phone to make a sale, the customer will more than likely say "yes."

How to Present Powerful Proposals That Sell

Remember that phone sales works with only one of your customer's information processing channels, and that most customers internalize less than one-third of what you say to them. Follow up with a written proposal when the situation warrants it, to help ensure that you have sealed the close.

To Prepare

1. Have all your needs assessment questions answered by the customer.

2. Have your ideas clearly thought out and understood so that you can present them in the best light.

3. Have the customers' names spelled correctly.

4. Make sure you know who is to receive copies of the proposal.

5. Use the customer's company colors somewhere in the binder, and as often as possible. (For example, if the customer is the Coca-Cola company, use red binders, etc.)

6. Focus on the customer benefits throughout the proposal. (For example, "What this means to you is . . .")

7. Give customers options so that they can make decisions based on variations of *your* company's product offerings.

8. Make the proposal as accessible and interesting as possible. Consider the following ideas:

   - Use a 12-point font for ease of reading.
   - Use colored paper in some places, but don't overdo unless it's for a visual arts type proposal.
   - Use graphics, illustrations, and color—again, don't overdo, but a simple bar or bullets in blue ink can catch the eye of your reader.
   - Include sample materials: software screen capture, a piece of metal casing, etc.
   - Use colored tabs to make it easier to find information.
   - Remember to place headings at the beginning of each important information section. Decision makers are "skimmers."
   - Put the customer's name on the outside of the binder or folder.

9. Include an Executive Summary in your proposal: a brief one-page synopsis for the quick reader who is interested only in the bottom line. *Put this first* after the table of contents page.

10. Make sure you include customer benefits throughout the proposal.

Components of the Proposal

- Title Page
- Table of Contents Page
- Executive Summary
- Customer Applications
- Your Company's Capabilities and Solutions

- Completed Product Samples
- Product Specifics
- Frequently Asked Questions
- Recommendation
- References
- Appendixes

Let's take a closer look at each of these elements.

Table of Contents. Include the page numbers and the major tab headings on this page.

Executive Summary. This is important to any decision maker, but especially to the results-focused **A** and the impulsive **E**.

Customer Applications. This is where you put the situation analysis or needs assessment that you have prepared in the course of interviewing the customer. In this section, you'll provide the overview of the situation as described by the client. Think of this as your customer's problem area (but don't use the word "problem"; it's negative and may suggest an insult to the customer). If you're selling office furniture, this is where you describe an out-of-date reception area, an ergonomically unsuitable research department of ten employees, an executive office that needs updating and upgrading, or more. Include the emotion behind the problems (whoops, we mean "situations") to which the customer needs a solution. For example: "The president's office is in need of updating so that he can present the company in the best light, indicating a bright future of company prosperity." This is where you remind the customer of the needs *he* or *she* voiced in your qualifying. Use the customer's words from your notes to describe the situation (remember all those notes you took? This is why!); that way your "insights" into the problem will ring true.

Capabilities and Solutions. This is an important section, but one that salespeople frequently present poorly. The customer is not interested in your entire company's history, and a generic cut-and-paste from the company's public relations summary or stockholder's report will be seriously ho-hum. Use a razor-sharp editing mind to present *exactly* what the customer will need to solve the problem. Spotlight your company's particular expertise in the area where the customer is most concerned. Here also you will be able to direct the customer to the appendix, where you have strategically placed a few positive articles about your company or the product/service the customer will be purchasing.

In addition, be sure to detail what the situation will be like when your product or service is put into use: "The order processing department will increase order turnaround by 50 percent when the optical character readers are used."

Product Samples. This is what the customer will have when done.

Product Specifics. Use a great amount of detail for technical customers, more "what it can do" for business decision makers who are less technical.

Frequently Asked Questions. Because you get questions regularly from customers, you have a clear sense of which ones are most prevalent in your industry. Spend some time thinking about this, and list and address them—but keep it brief. You might want to run this section past one of your colleagues after you have drafted it; he or she may have some excellent suggestions you can incorporate. It's well worth the time you spend on getting these right, as you can cut and paste this section into any proposal you write, as long as you remember to then tailor it to the situation at hand.

Recommendation. This is where you list the specifics of what the customer is buying. When you include a place to sign, the customer can send this part back to you as a purchase agreement, saving you and your customer time later.

References. Good references are important when the sale is competitive. By including happy customers in this section, you are providing an immediate shortcut to your decision makers' pocketbook. However, note that if you work in an industry where seeing a competitors' name is a negative, you may want to think carefully about which ones to include.

Appendix. Here's where you put articles in industry publications about your company or its products, also more details of tables or test results, etc., than you had room for in your proposal body. If you are pitching to a **P**, include plenty of test data, engineering specs, and even third-party white papers. (Note: If your firm doesn't have white papers, there are companies that will professionally write them for you.)

Now get on your phone and sell!

Index